Truth & Beauty

ALSO BY ANN PATCHETT

*Bel Canto*
*The Magician's Assistant*
*Taft*
*The Patron Saint of Liars*

# Truth & Beauty

*A Friendship*

## ANN PATCHETT

HarperCollins*Publishers*

The author and publisher thank the family of Lucy Grealy for the use of her letters.

HarperCollins books may be purchased for educational, business, or sales promotional use. For information, please write: Special Markets Department, HarperCollins Publishers Inc., 10 East 53rd Street, New York, NY 10022.

FIRST EDITION

*Designed by Amy Hill*

Printed on acid-free paper

Library of Congress Cataloging-in-Publication Data

Patchett, Ann.
   Truth & beauty : a friendship / Ann Patchett.—1st ed.
     p.  cm.
   ISBN 0-06-057214-0
   1. Grealy, Lucy. 2. Ewing's sarcoma—Patients—United States—
Biography. 3. Disfigured persons—United States—Biography.
4. Patchett, Ann—Friends and associates. 5. Grealy, Lucy—Friends
and associates. 6. Female friendship—United States. I. Title: Truth
and beauty. II. Title.

RD661.G74P386 2004
362.196'994716'092—dc22
[B]                               2003067586

04  05  06  07  08  ❖/RRD  10 9 8 7 6 5 4 3 2 1

Nothing lasts, and yet nothing passes, either.
And nothing passes just because nothing lasts.

—Philip Roth, *The Human Stain*

LUCINDA MARGARET GREALY

JUNE 3, 1963–DECEMBER 18, 2002

*Pettest of my pets*

# Truth & Beauty

## Chapter One

T HE THING YOU CAN COUNT ON IN LIFE IS THAT
Tennessee will always be scorching hot in August. In 1985 you
could also pretty much count on the fact that the U-Haul truck you
rented to drive from Tennessee to Iowa, cutting up through Missouri,
would have no air-conditioning or that the air-conditioning would be
broken. These are the things I knew for sure when I left home to start
graduate school. The windows were down in the truck and my stepsister, Tina, was driving. We sat on towels to keep our bare legs from
adhering to the black vinyl seats and licked melted M&Ms off our fingers. My feet were on the dashboard and we were singing because the
radio had gone the way of the air conditioner. "Going to the chap-el
and we're—gonna get mar-ar-aried." We knew all the words to that
one. Tina had the better voice, one more reason I was grateful she had
agreed to come along for the ride. I was twenty-one and on my way to
be a fiction writer. The whole prospect seemed as simple as that: rent a
truck, take a few leftover pots and pans and a single bed mattress from
the basement of my mother's house, pack up my typewriter. The hills of
the Tennessee Valley flattened out before we got to Memphis and as we
headed north the landscape covered over with corn. The blue sky
blanched white in the heat. I leaned out the window and thought,
Good, no distractions.

I had been to Iowa City once before in June to find a place to live. I was looking for two apartments then, one for myself and one for Lucy Grealy, who I had gone to college with. I got a note from Lucy not long after receiving my acceptance letter from the Iowa Writers' Workshop. She said that initially when she heard I had gotten into the workshop she was sorry, because she had wanted to be the only student there from Sarah Lawrence. But then our mutual friend Jono Wilks had told her that I was going up early to find housing and if this was the case, would I find a place for her as well? She couldn't afford to make the trip to look herself and so it went without saying that she was on a very tight budget. I sat at the kitchen table and looked at her handwriting, which seemed oddly scrawny and uncertain, like a note on a birthday card from an elderly aunt. I had never seen her writing before, and certainly these were the only words she had ever addressed to me. While Lucy and I would later revise our personal history to say we had been friends since we met as freshmen, just for the pleasure of adding a few more years to the tally, the truth was we did not know each other at all in college. Or the truth was that I knew her and she did not know me. Even at Sarah Lawrence, a school full of models and actresses and millionaire daughters of industry, everyone knew Lucy and everyone knew her story: she had had a Ewing's sarcoma at the age of nine, had lived through five years of the most brutal radiation and chemotherapy, and then undergone a series of reconstructive surgeries that were largely unsuccessful. The drama of her life, combined with her reputation for being the smartest student in all of her classes, made her the campus mascot, the favorite pet in her dirty jeans and oversized Irish sweaters. She kept her head tipped down so that her long dark blond hair fell over her face to hide the fact that part of her lower jaw was missing. From a distance you would have thought she had lost something, money or keys, and that she was vigilantly searching the ground trying to find it.

It was Lucy's work-study job to run the film series on Friday and Saturday nights, and before she would turn the projector on, it was up to her to walk in front of the screen and explain that in accordance with the New York State Fire Marshal, exits were located at either side of the theater. Only she couldn't say it, because the crowd of students cheered her so wildly, screaming and applauding and chanting her name, "LOO-cee, LOO-cee, LOO-cee!" She would wrap her arms around her head and twist from side to side, mortified, loving it. Her little body, the body of an underfed eleven-year-old, was visibly shaking inside her giant sweaters. Finally her embarrassment reached such proportions that the audience recognized it and settled down. She had to speak her lines. "In accordance with the New York State Fire Marshal," she would begin. She was shouting, but her voice was smaller than the tiny frame it came from. It was no more than a whisper once it passed the third row.

I watched this show almost every weekend. It was as great a part of the evening's entertainment as seeing *Jules et Jim*. Being shy myself, I did not come to shout her name until our junior year. By then she would wave to the audience as they screamed for her. She would bow from the waist. She had cut off her hair so that it was now something floppy and boyish, a large cowlick sweeping up from her pale forehead. We could see her face clearly. It was always changing, swollen after a surgery or sinking in on itself after a surgery had failed. One year she walked with a cane and someone told me it was because they had taken a chunk of her hip to grind up and graft into her jaw.

We knew things about Lucy the way one knows things about the private lives of movie stars, by a kind of osmosis of information. I do not remember asking or being told. It was simply passed through the air. Not only did we know about Lucy's childhood, her cancer, her bravery, everyone in school knew that Lucy was the poet. Better than a

very good college poet, she was considered by both teachers and hip-
sters to be a serious talent. She was always picked to give readings in
the coffee shop on Parents' Weekend. People pressed into the little
room to listen, her voice as small as it was when she directed us to the
emergency exits on Friday nights, but more self-confident.

"When I dream of fire," she read, "you're still the one I'd save /
though I've come to think of myself / as the flames, the splintering
rafters."

As I sat in the audience, watching, I believed we had something in
common even though I wrote short stories. People liked my work but
had trouble remembering me. I was often confused with another writer
named Anne who was in one of my classes, and with a girl named
Corinna who lived downstairs from me. Unlike Lucy, I had a tendency
to blur into other people. I had come to Sarah Lawrence from twelve
years of Catholic school where we were not in the business of discover-
ing our individuality. We dressed in identical plaid skirts, white
blouses, saddle oxfords, and when we prayed, it was together and
aloud. It was impossible to distinguish your voice from the crowd.
There is an art to giving yourself over to someone else and as a group
we mastered it. While Lucy had discovered that she was different from
all the other children in her grade school because she was sick and was
different from all the other children on the hospital's cancer ward
because she continued to survive, I had discovered I was so much like
every other little girl in the world that it always took me a minute to
identify my own face in our class photo. Still, I thought, in my shyness,
my blurriness, it would not be so unreasonable to think that the
famous Lucy Grealy and I could be friends. But when I waved to her in
passing or said hello in the cafeteria, she would look at me blankly for
a minute and then turn away as if we had never met. Once I stopped
her at the window where we returned our trays and dirty dishes.

"My father and stepmother live in Los Angeles," I said. "They invited a couple of the midshipmen from the Naval Academy over for Thanksgiving dinner and it turns out one of them went to high school with you. His name was Bobby something."

She stared at me as if she could not possibly imagine why I was speaking to her. I made another stab at my story. "I guess Sarah Lawrence came up and they figured out we both went there, so he asked my parents to ask me to tell you hello." I gave her a little smile but it went nowhere. "So, hello."

"Okay," she said, and walked away.

Lucy Grealy was much too cool for the likes of me, a girl from Tennessee who did not go to clubs in the city.

I graduated from college early and went back home to Nashville. When I got Lucy's letter, I never considered telling her no, she could find her own place to live. Lucy had the pull of celebrity, and while she had always ignored me, I was flattered to be asked for help. Besides, she would be the only person I knew in Iowa. I borrowed my mother's car and drove up in June to look at the cut-up houses and makeshift rooms used to store graduate students through hard winters. I quickly found that there was not a single apartment Lucy could afford, nor was there a single apartment I could afford. There were very few that we could have managed if we pooled our resources, and so I rented the only practical thing I could find, half of a very ugly green duplex on Governor Street for $375 a month, where we could at least have our own bedrooms. When I got home, I wrote Lucy and told her we would be roommates. It was not one of the options she had given me, but the numbers spoke for themselves. Neither of us could manage more than $200 a month.

I never thought that there was anything brave about moving to another state to live with someone I barely knew and yet suspected didn't like me, any more than it would have seemed hard to be broke and in pursuit of such an unlikely profession. Because my life had no shape, I was willing to accept whatever happened. If Tina had turned to me in that scorching U-Haul and said, Let's keep the truck, let's drive though Canada and take the Alcan Highway to Alaska, I probably would have been thrilled. Tina was good company and I very much wanted her to stay with me, but she was planning on her own adventure, riding her bicycle across America as soon as she dropped me off. Besides, by the time we made it to Iowa City, we were tired of the truck. We were sticky from sweat and all the candy we had eaten on the way. As we turned onto Governor Street, Lucy pulled up in the passenger seat of a gorgeous antique convertible driven by a handsome man. She waved ecstatically. "I'll be right there!" she called, and then they zoomed away.

I thought that things must be going well for Lucy.

The front door of the house was open wide. The living room was completely empty and the linoleum floor was shining wet and smelled of Pine Sol. I walked into the room, leaving a trail of footprints behind me.

"Did it look like this when you rented it?" Tina asked.

It looked like a storage unit. "I think it got worse."

We weren't there five minutes before Lucy was back. When I turned around to say hello, she shot through the door with a howl. In a second she was in my arms, leaping up onto me, her arms locked around my neck, her legs wrapped around my waist, ninety-five pounds that felt no more than thirty. She was crying into my hair. She squeezed her legs tighter. It was not a greeting as much as it was a claim: she was staking out this spot on my chest as her own and I was to hold her for as long as she wanted to stay.

"What happened?" I said, and I put my arms around her back.

There was never such a little back, and I felt it heave and sob. A bird in the hand. I thought something horrible must have happened. Only something truly outside of my understanding of bad things could drive this girl into my arms.

She pulled back to look at me. She kissed me and smiled and cried again. "I'm so glad you're here," she said.

I do not remember our love unfolding, that we got to know one another and in time became friends. I only remember that she came through the door and it was there, huge and permanent and first. I felt I had been chosen by Lucy and I was thrilled. I was twenty-one years old and very strong. She had a habit of pitching herself into my arms like a softball without any notice. She liked to be carried.

*Dearest anvil* [she would write to me six years later], *dearest deposed president of some now defunct but lovingly remembered country, dearest to me, I can find no suitable words of affection for you, words that will contain the whole of your wonderfulness to me. You will have to make due with being my favorite bagel, my favorite blue awning above some great little café where the coffee is strong but milky and had real texture to it.*

Lucy had mopped the floor three days before in honor of my impending arrival but the air in the duplex was so hot and humid and utterly motionless that the water and Pine Sol had simply puddled and stayed. For three days she had been waiting for me in the dampness.

"I thought you were never going to get here," she said. She was still holding on to my arm, even though her feet were now on the floor.

"How long have you been here?"

"Weeks, years. This place is horrible." She didn't say it unkindly, just as a statement of fact.

"Horrible," Tina said, nodding in sympathy.

"It was all I could find," I said, but I still felt guilty. "I'm going to get some things out of the truck."

"No," Lucy said. "We have to talk. There's too much I have to tell you." It was as if I were her oldest friend in life, just stumbling in through the door after ten years lost in Borneo.

The three of us went and sat on her bed on the floor. This was the story she told: On her first night in town she had gone to the local auction, where farmers who were going bust came to sell whatever they had left. She bought a futon mattress, a rug, a rickety table with chairs for the kitchen, and a grocery sack full of Harlequin Romance novels from the fifties, whose covers she planned to tear off and use to paper the bathroom. Then she promptly ran out of money.

"You're going to paper the bathroom in romance novels?"

"No, no, listen to me," she said, her voice high with excitement. "I met somebody. The guy in the car. I had sex."

B—— was twice her age and drove her home from the auction in his antique Jaguar convertible, whose turn indicators were two small flags that shot up from either side of the car and waved to establish the driver's intentions. Such charming turn indicators, coupled with a little attention, was all the reason Lucy needed. After a brief courtship in which he lent her several interesting books, they had sex. She was twenty-two and thrilled to be relieved of the burden of her virginity. In fact, she told me and Tina, it hadn't just been losing her virginity, it was solid experience. She had managed to sleep with him regularly since then.

"We'll go to the auction," she said. "I'll introduce you."

We went in the U-Haul, which didn't need to be turned in until the next day, and parked in the rutted grass. In a long barn there were cafeteria-style tables set out with boxes. One contained seven dolls with plastic heads and matted hair, four chipped cups, a coil of rope, pulleys, and two spades. The next had a toaster and a thick stack of record albums, half a dozen extension cords, several packs of playing cards, countless forks. Every box was an inexplicable collection of items that had to be purchased as a unit. There was no picking out what you wanted. Past the boxes were chairs and blankets and paintings of birds, an impressive assortment of Crock-Pots. Farmers and wives and children made slow loops around the tables, carefully studying what was available. They only raised their eyes from the merchandise to gawk at Lucy.

GAWKING IS A LOOK stronger than a stare. The gawk was full of brazen curiosity, pity, and fear, every unattractive human emotion rolled into one unflattering facial expression. If she saw them, and she must have since this was not a discreet spy job, she didn't let on. She had on shorts and a little red bowling shirt, dingy Keds. Up and down the aisles she held my hand. She was happy to be in Iowa, happy that Tina and I had arrived, happy she had a lover, even if we saw no sign of him that night. But I couldn't stop seeing those people. People who, had you set them down anywhere on the island of Manhattan, would have received some vicious gawking themselves. I would stop and stare at them until they noticed me. I would hold their eye for the seconds it took to make their faces warm and then watch as they scuttled outside to look at the heavy machinery. It was a trick I learned a long time ago, when I was nine years old, the year my sister and I were in the car accident. I remembered what it was like having people double back in the grocery store to get another look. Until the gawkers swung by for the third time, and then the fourth, I hadn't really understood how badly I'd been hurt. My sister, Heather, had been seriously injured and stayed in the hospital for another month after I was wheeled out to the pickup area. My problems, I had been told by family and doctors, were mainly cosmetic. My nose was broken, my lower lip had been torn through and reattached, my long hair had been cut off because it was too matted with blood, my face and neck were solid purple and green. I had a fractured wrist and a fractured skull. Shards of glass worked their way out of my head and through my hair for months. I was forever pricking my finger when I reached up to scratch my scalp. But sharp sudden headaches could not compete with the people who were looking at me. When I went back to a plastic surgeon at nineteen to have my nose rebroken and set again and the lower half of my face dermabraded off to lessen the scars (a second accident had sliced open my right cheek), I had not accounted for the fact that the world's tedious curiosity would be mine all over again, that it wasn't only battered-looking children that gawkers settled on.

*Oh*, people like to say when they hear this part of the story, *this is why you and Lucy are so close. You went through the same thing.* But nothing could be farther from the truth. I read one slim volume of the available information. Lucy read the library. My experience only left me smart enough to comprehend my own stunning lack of comprehension. When, as a child, I returned to school after a two-week absence, one of the older nuns took me aside to tell me that they were still offering the mass for my sister every day. Her superior grades had merged with her superior injuries and while she was plugged into a respirator she seemed to be a candidate for beatification. "God knew she was stronger than you," the nun told me. "That's why she was in the front seat. Because she had more grace, she was allowed to endure more pain." In short, it was God's love that had crushed my sister's larynx and His disappointment in my weakness that had let me off with comparatively so little damage. Even in the third grade I found this reasoning suspicious. I wasn't in the front seat because my sister was three and a half years older and had never let me sit in the front seat, not once, when she was in the car. There was no lesson there about God's love.

THE FIRST WEEK we were in Iowa, another student in the fiction program finally got up her nerve to ask me the question she had been wondering all along: How I could stand to look at Lucy every day? "Lucy's great," she said, "but I'd find it too upsetting. I'd always be thinking about her face."

I told her I had no idea what she was talking about and then I left abruptly, hoping she would feel horrible for having said it. But then I wasn't a good person to ask. I had stopped noticing Lucy's face years before, seeing her in the cafeteria or walking up the hill to class, always in the center of the most popular students. Or I saw her onstage, saying her lines, being cheered for her poetry or her introduction to *The Wizard of Oz*. And even though I didn't know her then, I had seen her face change significantly over the years. I thought it had improved. Her lower jaw had been a ledge falling off just below her cheekbone when we started college, making her face a sharp triangle, but now the lines were softer. She couldn't close her mouth all the way and her front teeth showed. Her jaw was irregular, as if one side had been collapsed by a brutal punch, and her neck was scarred and slightly twisted. She had a patch of paler skin running from ear to ear that had been grafted from her back and there were other bits of irregular patching and scars. But she also had lovely light eyes with damp dark lashes and a nose whose straightness implied aristocracy. Lucy had white Irish skin and dark blond hair and in the end that's what you saw, the things that didn't change: her eyes, the sweetness of her little ears. In Iowa she wore a four-by-four gauze pad, folded once and taped to the left side of her face, and while it was strange at first, it actually gave her a nice balance. It made it look like whatever was wrong was temporary, in the process of being fixed, when it was in fact part of a synthetic prosthesis that had worn a hole in her skin and was poking through. I asked Lucy countless times to let me see, but she wouldn't. The pad stayed fixed in place.

Lucy always said it was better when people just came out and asked her what had happened. A straight question was preferable to the awkward avoidance. "If they have the nerve to ask me, I'll tell them the truth," she said. Unless of course they asked her on a bus, in which case she would lean in close and whisper, "Bus accident." Or "Plane crash" or "Car wreck," depending on the mode of transportation at the moment.

B—— never seemed to mind Lucy's face. He was giving her a chance she thought she was never going to get, and so she was committed to following his lead. The first lesson was obedience. She came home early most mornings looking rumpled and calm. She would pour a cup of coffee and sit down across from me at the table.

"Bondage," she would begin patiently, "is not about a desire to be dominated."

And so began our sexual education, with Lucy attending the demonstrations at night and me reading off her notes in the morning. I would make her a bowl of Cream of Wheat while she talked about pornography, fetish, and whatever had happened the night before.

For two people who didn't know one another, Lucy and I had a lot in common, not only friends and classes from college and a vaguely stunned feeling about having found ourselves in the Midwest, we also between us had about four hours experience with men. We had both made it through high school without a single date. We both had our first kiss from the same boy in college (a sainted and tender soul who must have made it his business to kiss the girls who would have otherwise graduated unkissed). We were younger than any other twenty-two-year-old girls in the world, still believing absolutely that there was nothing more important, more romantic, than Yeats. Lucy, of course, had lived a larger life than I had, and she had infinitely more flair. Not only had she suffered, she had danced in New York's finest transvestite clubs, sometimes on the tables, where she was again regarded as a sort of lovable mascot. She had had adventures that, if not sexual, were at least sexy. And now she was having sex.

B—— was a cautionary tale about being careful of what you wish for: he was handsome and bright and attentive. He picked up Lucy in his fancy car and drove her into town for ice cream and coffee and all of the other students saw them and talked about it, just the way she hoped they would. According to the reports I heard every day, he liked sex, providing her with as many experiences as there were ice creams to choose from. But B—— was never going to love Lucy, and he seemed to take a real pleasure in telling her so. As much as Lucy had spent her college years dreaming that someday someone would want to have sex with her, she was slowly figuring out that wanting sex was knotted together with wanting love. The more B—— insisted the two be separated, the more confused and desperate Lucy became. The only avenue she had with B—— was sex, and she tried frantically to use it to make him love her. It was a bad habit she established, and it stayed with her for the rest of her life, long, long after B—— was gone.

*Dearest Axiom of Faith* [she would write to me later from Scotland, telling me a story about coming home and not being able to reach either of the two friends she had locally], *It was a sorry sight, me standing there by the phone, racking my brain for someone to call. I was seized with a profound loneliness and sense of desperation. My first impulse was to go to bed and feel very sorry for myself, but I forced, and I mean forced, myself to go out to a blues band playing at a bar down the street. I decided that if I was going to feel sorry for myself, I should at least do it in public with a drink in my hand and blues in the background. I ended up being chatted up by this man, D—— and we got drunk and ended up trying to have sex on the beach in a rainstorm (unsuccessful). He came back here with me and it was strange. He's in his mid-30's and was dumped by some woman he was desperately in love with only a few months ago. He's from aberdeen but lives in london. He was up here for the holidays, but was supposed to go back already, but kept putting it off because he was too depressed to face his job, which is for a shoe com-pany. The sex part was great—a real missionary sort of guy, but a great body. Oddly, he was like B—— in many ways: same sort of body, same body smell, a few of the same physical quirks: I felt like I was actually with B—— in a few ways. This was really great for me, for the fact that it'd been so long since I'd had sex, I'd begun to idealize the sex I'd had with B——, and this experience showed me he's a very replaceable per-son. I'm not sure the logic of that is too clear, but you can probably see what I'm getting at. The negative part of it was that he told me it wasn't physical attraction, but because of the conversation we'd had. He's all into spiritualism in a very new age sort of way, and I have to ashamedly admit I very proudly gave him all the soul-talk I knew. I'm ashamed of this because I took something very very important to me and used it as a device to get sex, and, worst, I talked about it in a way I knew to be (somewhat) false. I'm all for the roots of new-age and all that, but it seems to me too often confused with psychology and emotional happi-ness and self-awareness by certain types of people who are very sensitive and needy, yet not able to find what they want and need via art or more* traditional (and far more demanding and harder) philosophies and/or religions. Personally, I think true spiritualism contains aspects of the above mentioned things, but more often than not it shows you just how hard *things are, not how easy* (well, you know what I mean). Psychology wants you to adapt to society; spiritualism often tells you that you must not adapt (conform). Oh, anyway, this is all getting too jumbled. He was a very very sweet, very needy guy, who, after three nights, said he couldn't sleep with me any more because he didn't love me, and he was in a position in his life where he only wanted to make love, not just fuck. He went back on this when, after disappearing for four days he showed up again (still not having gone back to London) and we had another three nights of sex. I guess he's finally gone back now, or at least I haven't heard from him. We had some good conversations, and now he's gone I'm feeling very lonely, the way I did before I met him. It's like a big circle. I've gone on a get-a-man crusade, but so far it's been a disaster and I'm feeling as bad about myself as I ever have. I know I'm a great person and all that, a good friend, but I feel like real bottom of the barrel girlfriend material. D—told me I should do "affirmations," which is when you say positive things about yourself so as to posit them in the astral realm and counteract all the negative things you've ever said about yourself. In a weird way it makes sense (not the bit about the astral realm). Anyway, I'm trying very hard to be positive.

## Chapter Two

OUR RESPONSIBILITIES AT THE UNIVERSITY OF IOWA
were to be teachers and writers. While we had taken our writing very seriously through college, neither of us had ever considered
the prospect of teaching. I suppose we knew something about it simply
by virtue of having been in the room all those years when other people
were doing it, but at the time it seemed it would have been more provi-
dent to send us into the fields to husk corn as a means of reducing our
tuition to in-state rates. We had utterly no idea what we were supposed
to do on the other side of the desk. Lucy and I had both received the
same level of financial aid our first year, which meant we taught one
section of Introduction to Literature three days a week. There was a
week-long class before school started to prepare us for our new job,
but the only helpful piece of information we were given was the number of the room where we were to show up. Lucy and I went to our
empty classrooms, first hers, then mine, sat on the desks, and swung
our legs back and forth. The rooms were scorching hot.

"Is it over a hundred in here?" I asked.

Lucy looked at her shirt, which was already crumpled and damp.
"We're going to have to wear something that doesn't show sweat."

Two young girls leaned in the door. They looked like the sorority
sisters who marched up and down the sidewalk in front of our house

all day singing rush songs, "I'm a Kappa, we're a Kappa, here a Kappa, there a Kappa, wouldn't you like to be a Kappa, too?" High blond ponytails swinging to the Dr Pepper beat.

"Are you going to be in this class?" one of them asked.

We looked at them seriously for a minute and then we both started laughing, the impossible thought that we would have anything to teach these girls drove us into a terrifying state of hysteria.

We would have no supervision, no one to make sure that we weren't robbing the good children of Iowa blind with our ineptitude. We were told to pick a Shakespeare play, a contemporary play, two novels, five stories, and a dozen or so poems and spread them out over the course of the semester, issuing regular tests and paper assignments. I picked works that I knew well, but Lucy saw teaching as a great chance to further her own education. With the exception of the Shakespeare and the poetry, her syllabus consisted of things she had always meant to read.

The idea was, of course, that she would get around to reading them before she had to teach them, but somehow it never seemed to happen. She scanned the assignment while running to class, pages pressed down beneath her fingers. She figured as long as she managed to stay a few paragraphs ahead of the pack, she'd be all right. She maintained a strict policy that no one was to ask about the end of the book before the end had been assigned. "Alice," she would say sharply when Alice had ambitiously read too far beyond what was due, "it isn't fair of you to ruin it for everyone else in the class."

With or without reading the assignment, Lucy could power through a class on the sheer muscle of her oratory. She could talk. She could talk on the nature of truth and beauty for hours, and after all, what novel or poem or play in an Introduction to Literature class couldn't benefit from a truth-and-beauty discussion? She would often lie on the desk, half curled up, with her arm pillowing her head. She recited the ending of *King Lear* aloud, "Howl, howl, howl, howl! O, you are men of stones: / Had I your tongues and eyes, I'd use them so / That heaven's vault should crack. She's gone for / Ever! I know when one is dead and when one lives; / She's dead as earth."

Lucy loved *Lear*. She would have just as soon spent the entire semester on *Lear*.

"And then I would speak the two most beautiful words in the English language," she would tell me on the walk home. "Class dismissed."

*I bought The Iliad and Nabokov's Laughter in the Dark* [she wrote to me from the Bunting Institute at Radcliffe were she held a fellowship years later]. *The first is for a class I'm sitting in on, one taught by an absolutely genius professor: he dazzles me. Last week he did "Romeo and Juliet," which used to be my least favorite play. He changed my mind. He talked about how it's a play about the arbitrary accidental meetings in the street, arriving or waking up just one moment too late or too soon. From these moments of arbitrary "real" moments are forged by the characters through their own passions, which insist on taking moments in time and conditions of emotion that will eventually pass: anger, grief, and transforming them through actions into "forever," irrevocable conditions, such as through a curse on a family or a person, or by suicide. I still don't think it's my favorite play, but I do have new feelings about it. Monday I'll just have time for class before leaving for NY, he's doing the first four books of Homer, so I have to start reading. I'm ashamed to admit I've never read any of that stuff, unless you count the one or two abridged pages shoved down my unwilling throat in high school.*

My students, bearing up under the weight of my neatly typed syllabus and ironclad attendance policy, were certainly less enchanted than Lucy's students, but they always got their papers in on time. We were a pairing out of an Aesop's fable, the grasshopper and the ant, the tortoise and the hare. And sure, maybe the ant was warmer in the winter and the tortoise won the race, but everyone knows that the grasshopper and the hare were infinitely more appealing animals in all their leggy beauty, their music and interesting side trips. What the story didn't tell you is that the ant relented at the eleventh hour and took in the grasshopper when the weather was hard, fed him on his tenderest store of grass all winter. The tortoise, being uninterested in such things, gave over his medal to the hare. Grasshoppers and hares find the ants and tortoises. They need us to survive, but we need them as well. They were the ones who brought the truth and beauty to the party, which Lucy could tell you as she recited her Keats over breakfast, was better than food any day.

FOR US, IOWA was an abundant sea of time, hours and days and weeks to torch and burn. No matter how careless we were with our mornings and afternoons, there was more time, and then more. We spent hours over breakfast. Friends called and we would languish on the phone. Lucy was off to the gym to lift weights while I went to the pool and swam for so long I should have bumped my head on Cuba. We taught our classes, graded the papers, sat through office hours to talk to the young blond Iowan undergraduates who thought we were wise. We lingered in the hallways of the English and Philosophy building, running into people we knew, leaning against the cinder block walls to talk to them, until eventually Lucy and I would find one another and head off for drinks after work. That's how we liked to say it, because it sounded so grown-up: home from the office, off for cocktails. Happy hour featured three gin and tonics for the price of one, so that six glasses covered the dark glossy table of the booth. There was time to drink them all, though not before the ice had melted, and certainly someone we knew would see us there and slide in to order three more drinks for themselves.

"You have to wonder if Faulkner, Fitzgerald, and Hemingway knew the pleasures of three-for-one happy hour," Lucy said, pulling up the straw from her first glass.

"We are either following in a noble tradition or establishing one."

"Here's to not having a car." Lucy raised one glass out of six and I picked up another to clink against it.

Maybe one of us would wander away from the bar for an hour or so, a quick errand, the sight of someone we needed to speak to walking down the street, but when we came back, there the other would be, waiting, trying to read in the dim light of a fake Tiffany lamp. It was most likely to be me, and when she came back, I would look up and smile. "The return of the goose," I said. Later we would trip home for dinner, arms locked together against the cold, cutting through the park, stopping to swing on the swings. "What do you think?" I said, leaning back to look at the dark pink sky. "Snow?"

"I always wanted one of those ankles that predicted weather," she said. "Or an elbow. A snow elbow."

We had invented time, and we could not kill it fast enough. After dinner, dancing, and baths, we read, wrote our poems and stories, brushed our teeth, and tumbled into bed, only to find the next day was exactly the same. We had not moved one inch forward in the night. It was like prison, not in the punishment but in the vast sameness of the days. We were impossibly rich in time, and we lavished the excess on one another.

We shared our ideas like sweaters, with easy exchange and lack of ownership. We gave over excess words, a single beautiful sentence that had to be cut but perhaps the other would like to have. As two reasonably intelligent and very serious young writers in a reasonably serious writing program, we didn't so much discuss our work as volley ideas back and forth until neither of us was sure who belonged to what. Not that it mattered. Since we didn't share a genre, we could both find plenty of space inside the same idea. Lucy was always scrawling notes for poems on paper towels in the kitchen. I found a napkin by the phone that said "The Path to the Spiders' Nest" in her own spidery handwriting. "I love this." I held the napkin up when she came home. "I want this one."

"Too late," she said. "That one's taken." It was a note to remember to pick up an Italo Calvino novel I had never heard of before. I told her the plot of a story I was working on, about a magician's assistant whose magician is able to create the perfect illusion only in her dreams, but before I could finish it she wrote a poem called "The Magician's Assistant's Guilty Dream." I stole it back years later, when I wrote a novel called *The Magician's Assistant*.

"Many years later, as he faced the firing squad, Colonel Aureliano Buendia was to remember that distant afternoon when his father took him to discover ice," Lucy said to me one night when I came home from class. I stood in the doorway in my coat, scarf, hat, and gloves, shivering. "At that time Macondo was a village of twenty adobe houses, built on the bank of a river of clear water that ran along a bed of polished stones, which were white and enormous, like prehistoric eggs. The world was so recent that many things lacked names, and in order to indicate them it was necessary to point."

"You're memorizing *One Hundred Years of Solitude*?"

"I just want to try and get the first couple of pages," she said.

And so I unwrapped myself from the endless layers of winter protection and lay down on the rug, coaching her while she learned her lines.

I had read Marquez, but I had never tried to commit him to memory. I stayed with fiction and poetry while she went through philosophy and film criticism and the heavy art history books she lugged home from the library. She loved science. She took me to hear Stephen Jay Gould and we sat on the floor in front of him in a packed lecture hall while he made sensible links between fossils and baseball. That was Lucy's particular genius as well: the ability to take the disparate subjects she read about and find the ways that each one informed the other. I loved to listen to her talk. I was never happier than on the nights we stayed home, lying on the living room rug. We talked about classes and poetry and politics and sex. Neither of us were in love with the Iowa Writers' Workshop, but it didn't really matter because we had no place else to go. What we had was the little home we made together, our life in the ugly green duplex. We lived next door to a single mother named Nancy Tate who was generous in all matters. She would drive us to the grocery store and give us menthol cigarettes and come over late at night after her son was asleep to sit in our kitchen and drink wine and talk about Hegel and Marx. Iowa City in the eighties was never going to be Paris in the twenties, but we gave it our best shot.

IF I IMAGINE the artists in Paris, I do not see them dusting. I believe they were probably too engaged in the creative process to wrestle with such lowly concepts as coat hangers. Unlike Lucy, I could never give myself so completely over to my art that I would not notice the half-eaten plate of spaghetti in the middle of the living room floor. After a few early discussions it was agreed that my standard of acceptable cleanliness was something she would never be able to comprehend and I was unable to live at the level of squalor in which she seemed quite comfortable. The fact that she had mopped the floor before I arrived at the house on Governor Street marked her first and last attempt at housekeeping in the time we lived together. The compromise was that I would do all the cleaning and cooking and that neither of us would complain about it, which suited both of us fine. I stayed out of her bedroom, unless all of the glasses and plates had migrated there, leaving us nothing to eat off. For meals I made what we referred to as "Lucy-Food," a steady diet of things that did not have to be chewed: soft lasagna and half-done pancakes, biscuits and jelly, crushed graham crackers and instant coffee beaten into bowls of soft ice cream. Eating was a constant ordeal for Lucy, who had lost all of her lower teeth and all but six of her upper teeth during the relentless radiation treatments of her childhood. Her saliva glands had been damaged and she needed constant sips of water to get the food down. Her throat was scarred from years of surgical intubation, and that, coupled with her inability to put her lips together, meant she was forever choking on the smallest spoonful of pudding. On top of everything else, she had no feeling in her lower lip and chin and was mortified at the idea of having food all over her face and not knowing it, which was often the case. When Lucy went out to dinner with other people, she would usually sit and sip a beer, waiting until she came home to eat. I would overcook her spaghetti and then she would mince it, crosshatching her knife and fork across her plate again and again and again, the clacking of the metal banging out an assault of cutlery against food. When the spaghetti was pulverized into a totally unrecognizable version of itself, she would begin the long task of eating what she could, which, in light of all the effort, was never much. By the end she was red-faced and sweating, exhausted by dinner. Still, she liked the fact that she always sat at a table and ate with a napkin. She thought it was civilized. Even though she couldn't have walked down the street eating a piece of pizza, she said she wouldn't have wanted to.

After the dishes were washed and put away, Lucy put a tape in the little stereo box and we danced in the kitchen. No matter how dismal things seemed, ungraded papers, brutal weather, we could find the energy to spin around the table under the bright fluorescent lights of our apartment. Lucy was a brilliant dancer and I was tireless in my efforts to imitate her. "Just concentrate on the waist down," she said. "Take it half a body at a time." But when that proved to be too much for me, she narrowed it again. "Okay, just work the right foot." I held my arms over my head and rolled my foot to one side and then the other, following her. In college, Lucy had been the queen of the dance marathons, dancing every song in groups, alone, with a circle of people around her, marveling. She moved like water, the embodiment of easy rhythmic confidence, while I hung against the wall. Sarah Lawrence specialized in a mix of talent and exhibitionism that made it impossible for novices to take their place on the floor. Kitchen dancing was the only hope for girls like me who needed to find their way in privacy. On Governor Street we would dance for hours. We laughed so hard and the music was so loud that some nights our neighbor Nancy had no choice but to come over and dance with us for a while. We danced until our hair was damp and our feet ached from the linoleum floor, at which point Lucy would go and get in the tub (Lucy, skinny, was always freezing and could most easily be found in a hot bath). I would sit on the edge, sweaty and exhausted, smoking cigarettes.

"Look at this," Lucy said, grabbing the outside of her thigh. "Fat, fat, fat."

"On what planet?"

"You're not looking."

"You want to talk fat?" I would throw one leg up on the tub. "Look at this!"

Most people thought that Lucy's story was in her face, a history in the irregular line of her jaw, but it was her entire body. It had been systematically carved apart for its resources over the years: the skin and muscle taken from her back had left wide swaths of scar tissue; delicate, snaky scars wrapped around her legs because some surgeon had needed an extra vein; one hip had been mined for bone grafts and had left a spiky stalagmite peak that pushed threateningly against the ropy pink skin. In the future they would take her lower ribs and a bone from her leg and the soft tissue from her stomach and pour them all into her jaw, where they would gradually melt away into nothing. But while she was tortured by her relationship with her face and talked about it being ugly, she had a real fondness for her body. Every scar was a badge of honor, and she was always pleased to whip off her shirt to show someone the scars on her back and tell their unhappy story. She had a lack of physical modesty common to many people who had spent that much time naked in hospitals.

What she mulled over most nights in the tub, staring down at herself through the soapy water, was the state of being flat-chested. She took a wet washcloth and laid it over her ribs, pulling either side tight under her arms. "Nothing," she said. "Zip." I wanted to say it was otherwise, but I couldn't argue with her. There was no room for disagreement.

"There's nothing wrong with being flat-chested," I tried.

She sighed and hoisted herself out of the tub. "Spoken like a person with breasts," she said.

Lucy had had radiation to her torso as a child and it had frozen her there forever, a permanent record of her eleven-year-old self. Since she had cut off her hair in college, she often passed as a young boy, her shoulders rolled forward, hands shoved deep in her pockets, the collar of her ratty leather jacket turned up. But the pose always fell apart when the ticket taker at the movie theater said, "Yes, sir," and "Thank you, sir." Then she came home crying. Lucy didn't want to be a boy; she wanted to be a girl who would be seen as especially sexy in her boyishness. She wanted to be Jean Seberg, *la gamine*. B—— was suggesting that she should perhaps consider cultivating a different kind of sexiness, something more feminine and traditional than the James Dean look.

Lucy started doing a kind of superfast jogging in place in the living room that made her look like she had plans to try out for the Hawkeye football team.

"What's this about?"

"It's what the girl in *Flashdance* did and she had the best legs," she said, panting but not stopping. "I figure ten minutes a day."

Lucy didn't work out in the living room for long. She joined the fancy gym in town. She went to the mall and bought a pair of black stockings and a garter belt. A few days later we went back for a pair of high heels and a short skirt. Then some shorter skirts. Despite her grousing about her upper thighs, Lucy had wonderful legs, and it wasn't long after her initiation into femininity that she made the decision to get some wonderful breasts to go with them.


MY FAMILY, like every family, had its own particular set of insanities about money, but we had enough. In certain instances, we had too much. I don't remember anyone ever crying over stacks of bills. My family paid for me to go to college and then I said that I would make it through graduate school on my teaching assistantship. It was a point of honor, and my stepfather, who was thrilled that I wanted to be a writer, was actually irritated with me for not letting him pay for this new degree. At the end of every month I was down to about forty-five cents, and while I didn't call home to ask for money, I could have, and that knowledge made all the difference. Lucy, on the other hand, had grown up in a whirlwind of financial crisis. She believed she was poor and that she would stay poor and for the most part she didn't worry about it. Her past was littered with hospital bills that would never be paid. She had taken out huge student loans as an undergraduate, figuring they would probably go the way of her hospital bills. She took out loans for Iowa, which gave her more of a cushion even though she also had a teaching assistantship. So when she decided that breasts would be the best accessory to go along with her new skirts and heels, she simply took out another government loan.

"You're a poet," I said. "How do you think you're going to pay this off?"

"I'll worry about it later."

I followed her through the apartment and into her bedroom. "You're going to be swallowed alive by debt."

Lucy sighed at my stupidity. "You don't pay off what you borrow. You cut some kind of a deal with them. You tell them what you're going to give them and they take what they can get."

Was it possible that people worked out the details of how they were going to shirk off their debt before they ever borrowed the money?

Lucy knew I didn't get it. I didn't get the envelopes she never opened, or her stories about going up and down the halls at the Plaza Hotel in college and taking food off of room-service trays, a hobby born out of a peculiar sense of down-and-out glamour rather than actual hunger. I did not get her occasional habit of sticking a book of poetry under her jacket when we went to readings at the local bookstore late at night. I was of the bourgeois world of regular payments.

Twelve years of Catholic school had taught me that I would be held accountable not only for what I did, but for everything I considered doing. Twelve years of beating cancer had taught Lucy that she was invincible and that nothing, none of it, was ever going to catch up with her. She had a sense of superiority where money was concerned. She believed that not having any had made her worldly and wily, in the same way she believed that coming from the suburbs had branded me forever as naive.

"The difference isn't who has what in their checking account," she said. "The difference is the safety net. If you bottom out, you have people who'll rescue you. If I bottom out, it's a free fall."

I shook my head. "That's completely stupid. You have the exact same safety net that I do. You have me."

When the loan came through, there was only enough for saline implants, not the fancier silicone ones she had hoped for, but Lucy accepted the compromise. The waiting room of the plastic surgeon's office in Cedar Rapids was small and dark with pine paneling and we watched the fish swim back and forth in the tank because the magazines were bad. Based on my limited personal experience, I had thought it was a given that plastic surgeons had good magazines. After the examination, the doctor said he would have to order special implants for Lucy, something smaller than the smallest size they had. Lucy was pleased. Something smaller than the smallest meant she was special, a patient unlike any of the other patients who were probably just greedy anyway, people who already had breasts and now wanted bigger ones. "They should be tasteful," she said.

That was the first surgery I went through with Lucy, the introductory course, and it was a breeze, a fairy story of getting what you dreamed. She came home feeling fine, her chest swaddled like a newborn. She shook her bottle of Tylenol III and smiled. For a couple of days she was careful not to lift her arms too high or pick up anything heavy. When she took off the dressing it was more like an unveiling, and everyone was welcome to come over and see. We all agreed they were dazzling, the perfect breasts of a slim fifteen-year-old, the very ones that jaw cancer had inadvertently cheated her out of years before. She was hopelessly in love with them. This was plastic surgery: a wish, a government loan, a dream come true. All of those other surgeries, the painful, wretched failures of her childhood, were not the absolute rule. Sometimes things work out exactly the way the doctor says. Now there was proof. "The best part of my student loans," she would say for years, cupping one small breast in each hand. "The best thing I ever got out of graduate school."

We were in the habit of borrowing cars in those days; usually it was Nancy's, whose vacuum cleaner I also relied on heavily. But on the day the stitches were to come out, Nancy had an appointment and so I borrowed an old Toyota and Lucy and I headed back to Cedar Rapids. When we had made it half of the way there, the car died on the interstate. It started to snow, a light dust blowing over the blacktop, and then it snowed harder. We set off walking backwards, thumbs out, trying to hitchhike to the postoperative breast augmentation appointment, perhaps a first in the state of Iowa. There were very few cars on the road, and the one that stopped for us was the least promising of all, a rusted-out 1970 Honda Civic that had probably been red at some point and had long since turned the shade of dried blood. It shivered beside us on the road as the woman in the passenger seat rolled down her window and asked us where we were going. The driver, a man too large to have squeezed into the car in the first place, leaned around her, his dark beard flecked with sugar.

"The hospital," Lucy said. She was still wearing the gauze pad taped to the missing side of her jaw and it gave our request a kind of gravity that the truth would have lacked. The woman nodded and leaned forward so that we could crawl into the tiny backseat. It was full of white Styrofoam flats covered in wisps of Saran Wrap, half-eaten jelly doughnuts flattened inside. We tried to keep from sitting on the doughnuts and instead sat on the empty trays. Lucy and I held hands and pressed our knees together, both of us wondering if we had just made a very serious mistake.

"Awful cold," the man said. The woman scooted down in her seat.

"Yes, sir," I said.

"You girls pick up hitchhikers?"

"I do," Lucy said, meaning that if she had a car she certainly would.

He nodded and we watched the back of his head, his long ponytail caught up in a greasy knot. "I tried to hitch from Chicago to Cedar Rapids one time," he told us. "Didn't have enough money for a bus ticket. I started walking on the interstate and not one person stopped for me. Nobody. Ended up having to walk the whole way. It took me three days and I'll tell you, it was cold. Not one person cared if I needed help."

We were all silent. I didn't know whether or not I should apologize, since I was sure I wouldn't have picked him up either.

"You got to stop for people," he said, punctuating every word. "That's what you owe me for this ride. You have to pick somebody else up. Do you understand me? Pick them up no matter what they look like."

## Chapter Three

WHEN LUCY WAS FOUR, HER FAMILY CAME TO
America from Dublin with her two sisters and two brothers.
Her father had been one of the first television journalists in Ireland and
his popularity there had landed him a good job with a major network
in New York. Lucy's father died of pancreatitis when she was fourteen,
and she kept a black-and-white photograph of him on the wall in the
living room. He was wearing a trench coat and smoking a cigarette and
he looked straight ahead at the camera. He managed to cut a figure
that was at once both dashing and endearing. His eyes were Lucy's
eyes. She was in no way sentimental about her family, but the picture
was there like a soft spot.

*Grief isn't something to 'be gotten through.' It has no life of its own like
that, it's just plain and simply there. It's one of the things which tells us
we're human. It's funny, but I'm always forgetting I had cancer. It seems
like a different person that happened to. I can never relate what I'm
going through now with cancer either, even though it is the only reason I
am here, in aberdeen. Lately the past haunts me a lot. It seems a day
does not go by in which I do not remember the chemotherapy, even
though once again it oddly doesn't seem to be connected with cancer. I
guess I just never really accepted having it, never thought about it. I look*

*back on that part of my life and I was in a continual state of despair, yet I remember it the same way you would remember any objective detail. I wore a red dress. I was in a state of despair. It wasn't me at all.*

*It's much the same with my father. Like the chemo he comes back to haunt me all the time, but it's often a detached sort of haunting. Or it is very emotional, very joyous. That might sound odd, but often I feel better able to live and love life through remembering my father. James Tate has a wonderful poem about his father called "The Lost Pilot" (also the name of the book); have you ever read it? It's about the advantages (I don't mean to be crude, using that word) of his father's early death, how now as an adult he realizes his father would already be dead, or very old and decrepit. I have a very pure image of my own father, one that is almost a myth. It has more to do with me than with him.*

When she got a call from a film producer in Ireland who had been a friend of her father's, she was very pleased. It was someone who knew him back in the days before they moved, back in the days that Lucy didn't exactly remember herself but believed marked a better time in the history of the Grealy clan. The producer knew about her story, the cancer, the surgeries, and he wanted to come to Iowa with a film crew to tape a short documentary about her life, the life of a twenty-two-year-old Irish girl who had overcome insurmountable odds.

"Are you serious?" I said.

"They told me the theme was 'The Triumph of the Human Spirit.'"

"That's you all right."

"The Triumph of the Human Spirit." She leaned forward and put her head against her skinny arms. "Oh my God, what have I done?"

Lucy didn't want to be known for her face. She wanted to be known for her poetry, for her ideas. Still, there was part of her that looked forward to the film crew. She liked the attention, she liked the fact that

they were coming from Ireland. She liked the thought of meeting someone who knew her father.

The film crew, when they arrived, consisted of three overly large
men with cameras and bags and lights packed into a small rental car.
When they unpacked their gear, it was impossible to imagine they
could have squeezed such an enormous amount of flesh and equipment
into such a tiny space or how they would ever cram it all back in again.
They were driving around the States putting together as many stories
as they could find before going home. They stood awkwardly in our
living room, which contained a single chair and a tiny foam-rubber
love seat that was completely unsuitable for anyone weighing more
than 130 pounds. The producer looked at the picture on the wall and
tapped the frame. "Ah, your dad was a great guy," he said. That was
all. Even I was hoping for something more. They were all looking hard
at Lucy, not just her face, but all of her. Would she be enough to fill up
a television screen?

"Come ride around with us," the producer said. "Show us the
sights."

"There aren't a lot of sights," Lucy said, but they all piled in the car
and drove away. I waved to them from the door, a worried mother
sending her daughter off to the prom with three dates.

When she came home late that night, she was quiet and tired. She'd
had dinner with the film crew and a couple of beers and then they
dropped her off on Governor Street and drove away.

"So," I said. "Are you going to be a movie star?"

Lucy left her coat in a pile on the floor. She fell down on the couch
and put her head in my lap. "I couldn't do it."

I brushed back her hair with my fingers and asked her why not.

"Oh, it was the whole Triumph of the Human Spirit thing. Every
time they talked about it, I couldn't stop laughing. It doesn't matter. I

don't think they wanted me anyway. I don't think I was what they had in mind."

I couldn't tell whether or not she felt bad about it, and I don't think she could tell either. It would be nice to be on television in Ireland, but not because of her face.

A few days later I went along with her to a lecture Jim Galvin was giving on Faulkner and in the middle of the class I tore a corner off a piece of paper, printed the word TRIUMPH, and slipped it over to Lucy. When she read it, she started to sputter a little, then giggle. She tamped it down for a minute or two, but then it came back. At first she had a hold of it, but then it got out of hand, a little kitchen fire that suddenly rears back and swallows the house whole. The laughter was bigger than she was and there was simply no fighting it. By now the class had stopped, Galvin stopped, and we watched her as she choked and wept and laughed. "I'm sorry," she said, but she could barely make the words. She pulled her books together and left the room. I followed her. She tried to berate me but she couldn't stop laughing.

LUCY, NOT A TELEVISION STAR, occasionally a triumph, went back to work on her poetry, leaving drafts around the house the same way she left her scattered clothes. She gave me xeroxed copies of the poems she read and loved. She ripped pages out of literary magazines and taped them to the refrigerator. Poetry defined her, saved her. There were times it seemed to be the only thing around that made perfect sense.

*I'm getting really dependent on art, ann. That might sound pretentious, and it might very well be due to the fact that I'm in the midst of a bit of an emotional abyss at the moment, but it seems to be the only place I find any meaning. But the amazing thing, the most extraordinary thing to me, is that this meaning I find is itself totally undefinable. Just now this is especially true with painting. I've always in the past been a bit hot and cold about contemporary painting, yet in the last year or so it's begun to have a real effect on me. Painting styles I would have scoffed at before can now grab my attention and give me a real sense of . . . importance? (Not my own, theirs). I bought this giant book of contemporary american and german painting at a big discount, and I'm loving it. It makes me wish I were a painter. But poetry too, that's been really important to me lately, redefined, as it were. I could never stand John Ashbery before, but now I'm reading things of his which I love (though admittedly I still have great trouble with the bulk of his work). The whole point I'm trying to work up to is that I think, I am sure, that this new importance poetry and art in general is having for me has to do a great deal with my precarious emotional state. Does this raise or lower, then, the everyday importance of art? Does something which exists on the edge have no true relevance to the stable center, or does it, by being on the edge, become a part of the edge and thus a part of the boundary, the definition which gives the whole its shape? I would like to believe it is the latter, but does wanting to believe in something make that something valid? (Didn't they used to use this argument for the existence of god back in the olden days?)*

Had we managed to keep our lives focused on art, I think we would have lived in a state of brilliant happiness, but no one can stand in front of a painting forever. By the spring I was dating a fiction writer who was in love with another woman who had recently dropped him. He was very sad and would clearly benefit from my enthusiastic bolstering. It wasn't a good relationship, but at least I could now contribute to the morning's discussions of sex. Lucy kept on with B——, but they broke apart and came back together so many times they were like a plate that had been dropped on the floor repeatedly: more glue than china. Lucy tried to get out of it, but she could never quite bring herself to believe that B—— wasn't better than nothing at all.

"He's insane," she said. "Everything he says is insane, it's absolutely clear and I'm sure of it, but then he'll say one little thing that is so completely true that it undoes me. The true thing catches you off guard, and then everything starts to unravel, and you think about all the insane things he said and you start to wonder if maybe *they* were true too and maybe you just didn't want to believe it. That's what he's always telling me anyway, that I didn't believe the rest of it because I couldn't face the truth."

She told me the truth according to B—— was that she was always going to be alone, that no one would ever love her, and it wasn't because of the way she looked, it was because of who she was as a person.

Like any sensible friend, I told her not to listen. "The point isn't to hear it and then reject it. The point is to cross to the other side of the street when you see him coming." I told her what my father always said: if you don't want to engage with someone, don't engage with them, ever, on any level, and they will go away. But she was so hungry for attention and interpretation she would take it wherever she could get it. Lucy read her horoscopes studiously. She threw pennies on the kitchen floor and asked the I Ching for solid advice about her life.

One day B—— came and sat down with me at the Great Midwestern Ice Cream Company, the store from which he had brought us quarts of blueberry ice cream in the early days of his courtship with Lucy. He asked me how I was doing. I was doing okay. He and Lucy hadn't seen each other for a week or two at this particular point and I knew what she would want: she would want me to sit and listen. She would want me to go on a fact-finding mission. While B—— and I had been in the same room on many occasions, we had always been with Lucy, and I was curious to see what he would say if we were alone. I thought I could figure him out, break the code. I would take some necessary piece of information back to Lucy that would show her she should ditch this guy once and for all.

If B—— had been an actor, he would have been cast in the role of the handsome lobsterman. He had a straight nose and straight sandy brown hair. He was slim and well exercised and his convertible had left him with a casual glow of health, a little pink on top of his tan. He asked me how my work was going. He said that Lucy had told him I was dating someone. "Don't let it get in the way of your writing," he said. "That's the most important thing. That's the reason why you're here." B—— had been a student at the Writers' Workshop years before and he gave off the easy confidence of someone who had the inside track. He wanted to know how much I had written. Did I work every day? "It's got to be every day," he said. "If you don't turn out pages every day, you're not really a writer. You're just playing at it. You're wasting your time."

I didn't want to talk about me. I wanted to know what he had to say about my friend. I was not the topic of conversation.

"Oh, but you are," B—— said, as I took another nervous bite of ice cream. "If you're interested in being a writer, if you're for real. But you won't be for real if you don't write the pages. Then you're just like everybody else. A lot of talk and nothing ever gets done. All promise, no delivery, am I right?"

"I write," I said.

"Sure you do. Everyone does. You have some little story in your head that you're going to get around to. This town is full of those people. I see them come in wanting to be writers and winding up as waitresses. The

Workshop practically manufactures waitresses. What makes you think you're going to be different from anybody else? Are you different? Are you special?"

"I'm not special." What were we talking about?

"It's hard to say." He wagged his finger at me. "But it doesn't sound like you're doing the work. That guy you're seeing, he'll figure you out, too, then he'll drop you, because he'll know that you're not ever going to be the thing you say you're going to be, because you don't do anything, you aren't anything. You aren't the girl with all the promise, the girl who's going to be the real writer. He'll see that you're nothing, you're just something to fuck. Then he'll drop you, too."

At some point I stood up and walked out into daylight, leaving my ice cream there to melt on the table. I felt panicked, not that B—— would follow me, but that what he said would follow me, that his words had somehow attached themselves to me and were working their way into my clothing, burrowing down towards my skin like nettles. At twenty-two I felt like I had just received the worst tarot card reading in the world and I hadn't even asked for it. What if he was right? What if I was nothing? What if someone else had seen it?

When I got home I told Lucy everything, and she loved it. It gave her real comfort to know that I had seen him the way she saw him, and that it had scared me half to death.

B—— BERATED LUCY for her lack of sexual experience. He wanted her to sleep with other men, and so she did, half to get away from him and half in hopes of getting him back. Seduction was a quest, a skill, and a full-time job. The question was never whether or not Lucy wanted the man, the question was only whether or not the man wanted her. It was her truest hope that everybody wanted her. She had affairs with other students in the program, students outside the program, and one of the undergraduates in her literature class. In the course of a year she had gone from believing that she would die a virgin to thinking there was lost time to make up for. What she wanted was love, and the best way to go looking for it was through sex.

But it never worked that way, and the sex just made her lonelier. I understood that, as it had made me lonelier too. I couldn't ever remember being lonely before, certainly not in this way, until I had seen the edge of all the ways you could be with another person, which brought up all the myriad ways that person could never be there for you.

A FEW WEEKS later we went to see *Peggy Sue Got Married* at the mall downtown. Lucy and I were shameless about movies. We would see almost anything that allowed us to sit in the dark air-conditioning of a theater. The night had been fine when we went in, but now it was late and the rain was beating down in dark curtains. We sprinted across the street to a sports bar and took up a little table in the back, ordering drinks while we blotted our hair with thick stacks of paper napkins. There was some game playing on the ten television sets that hung down from the ceiling of the bar, and though there were very few women in the room, no one noticed us at all.

"My God, that was a bad movie," I said. "Nicolas Cage. What was he thinking?"

"I didn't hate it," Lucy said.

"Really?" I was going to tease her, but suddenly she was crying. "What is it?" I said quietly. We could have both sobbed out the darkest corners of our grief and no one in that bar would have known.

"They were together," she said. "It wasn't perfect, but they were together."

"Pet, it was a very stupid movie."

"I am always going to be alone," she said. Her hair was still wet. Her cheeks were wet. "I am never going to find someone."

"You're going to find someone."

"You don't understand." She folded her arms on top of the small table and put her head down to cry.

Lucy tried constantly to find and fully participate in any joy that was available to her, but still she was pulled into scorching bouts of depression. Her grief about feeling ugly and her desire to be loved in a way that would be huge enough to meet her needs would regularly roll her into a little ball and paralyze her. She would cry for hours and then for days. Lucy's sadness terrified me, in large part because it made such perfect sense. No matter how anyone argued for the virtues of her talent and her friendships, the many jewels of her life, there was no denying the fact that what she had been through and what was still ahead of her seemed insurmountable. The damage to her face was a fact, but over the years she had cemented that fact to the idea that she was unlovable. She would tell me that she would give it until winter, then she would go out to the cornfields wearing a light jacket at night, drink a bottle of whiskey, and lie down in the snow.

I put down my head as well and she turned to show me her wet blue eyes. "Listen to me. You will find someone. You always find people. You haven't found the right one yet, but no one has. You aren't going to be alone. You're going to have me."

A unified roar went up in the bar. A necessary point scored by the favored team, I could only assume. I put my hand on Lucy's back and felt her uneven breaths, the tremor of her shoulder blades. I was stunned by the rawness of her pain. I came to understand that night in the sports bar, safe from the blinding rain, that I could not worry about Lucy anymore. I knew then it was just too enormous for me to manage and that worrying about her would swamp me. If I was swamped by worry, I would be useless to her. It was even possible that I would desert her, and that was the thing that could never happen. I decided that night I would take all the hours of my life that could so easily be spent worrying and instead I would try to help her. I had been raised by Catholic nuns who told us in no uncertain terms that work was the path to God, and that while it was a fine thing to feel loyalty and devotion in your heart, it would be much better for everyone involved if you could find the physical manifestations of your good thoughts and see them put into action. The world is saved through deeds, not prayer, because what is prayer but a kind of worry? I decided then that my love for Lucy would have to manifest in deeds.

*Dearest Pet,*

*We had a little mini-blizzard here today. Snowflakes as big as 10p pieces and so plentiful you could barely see across the street. I was in the gym when it started, and rushed myself a bit so I could make it outside before it stopped. Unfortunately I didn't make it, but still, it was a new aberdeen, and I had fun walking around, thinking Gee, aberdeen actually looks pretty. Then I started thinking, Fuck, it's cold out, so I went to Café Drummond and sat in the back, drinking tea, reading a book I'd bought earlier. It's a big expensive book, my christmas present to myself, on the history of cinema, full of all sorts of snooty intellectual theories which I always find so entertaining. Maybe I'm just a common snob, or a pseudo-intellectual, but I really do get a kick out of that long-hair stuff. I left about 3:30, which is when the sun begins to set. The sky was clear, a sort of pale baby blue, and scattered in it were big cotton clouds; it wasn't just my clothes which were layered: it's amazing how many things we can think of at once: how pretty it was, how normally ugly it is, the theory of authorship versus genre, what a good workout I'd had,*

*how much I hated my ass, how I wish I could write better, you, B——,
David Madole, the other David I'm obsessed with, and, inexplicably,
Beth Filson. Only now, as I'm typing this, have I realized the only thing
I wasn't thinking of was how lonely I was. I guess I was my old self for
awhile there, my better self. Lately I've been completely obsessed by my
loneliness: it colors (note I didn't say colours) everything I see these past
few weeks. It's okay to be lonely, I know that, but I don't like the way
it's become the thing by which I measure everything else. I can't seem to
try to not be lonely: it only seems to happen accidentally, like this afternoon.*

On the cold mornings that we were both home, Lucy would get up
in the dark early hours and come into my room. "Scoot over," she said,
and I would press up against the wall beside my single bed and she
would crawl in beside me and wrap her arms around my waist. We
would lie in the warm flannel sheets and I would listen to the steady
sound of her breathing behind me. "Someday we'll look back on all of
this and we won't even believe we were here," she whispered. "We'll
say, 'Do you remember when we used to live in Iowa?'"

I smiled, warm, already falling back to sleep. I told her, "We'll say,
'That happened during the Iowa years.'"

Chapter Four

I DID LUCY AND MYSELF A GREAT DISSERVICE OUR second year at Iowa and left the house on Governor Street to move in with my boyfriend, who lived in a small cottage behind a larger house a mile away. This act of packing up and leaving home set in motion a much larger mistake that would take years to correct. At the time I thought this was my big chance for love, that I was doing something very romantic and important, but looking back on it now, it all seems part of a very simple equation: I left the house where I lived with someone who loved me to go to the house of someone who did not love me at all. Wasn't it more important to live with a man, a man who was certain to wake up one day and be happy because I was there with all my good intentions sleeping beside him? Wasn't that more valuable than staying with a friend who made me laugh, who made me think about everything, but was, in the end, just a girl? I shouldn't have had to choose between them. Lucy was devastated that I was going and she let me know it in no uncertain terms. I left her all my furniture and continued to pay my half of the rent for months until she could find a place of her own, but it didn't make any difference.

Of course, Lucy and I still saw each other all the time. Dennis had a television set and a VCR and the second he left the house I would call Lucy and she would come over so that we could do Jane Fonda videos together. It was the eighties, after all, and we were crazy about Jane Fonda.

*Pettest of my pets, There is a crisis in leadership. Rumours had been circulating, but I'd staunchly refused to believe them, but now I have had them confirmed by a reliable source (T.V. a.m.). Jane Fonda has had ribs removed, a la Cher. Is this true? I can't bring myself to believe it. What ramifications does this have for us? I am so terribly disappointed in her, though I also understand the mania twixt this ribectomy comes. After all, I'm about to have a sizable chunk of my pelvis carved off. Not the same thing, yet the same thing: spock would understand this logic even if no one else would. She had it all: the bod, the bucks, the film contracts: why did she resort to this madness? Is she afraid of something? What could it be? Are we afraid of the same thing, the same sort of thing, whatever it is? Promise me you will never let me have a rib removed, and I swear the same unto you. I forgive her til the end, yet something is different. Jane is as fallible as us: she always was, I know, but. . . . a pair of ribs! They don't grow on trees, you know.*

Lucy didn't just come over when Dennis was gone, she came over when we were both gone. She had a key to our house and if we were away for the night she usually managed to bring someone over to have sex in our bed. She always managed to tell me about it.

"Stop it," I said.

"We just came over to water the plants," she said innocently. "I didn't know it was going to happen."

EARLY THAT SPRING, Lucy and I went to have our fortunes told by a young, heavyset woman named Jan who lived in a duplex out in Cedar

Rapids with her three small children. She had a reputation for getting things right. We decided I would go first and she dealt out my tarot cards on the orange shag carpet of her small living room while Lucy and I sat cross-legged on the floor, waiting for the future. Jan carefully studied the bright pictures of cups and swords and moons, and when she had it all figured out, she smiled at me. "The man you're with now is the greatest love of your life," she said. "You will stay with him forever."

I was more than a little surprised but I took it as a good sign: things in my relationship would have to improve. Then Lucy scooted forward and Jan reshuffled the deck. Lucy cut the oversized stack and Jan dealt them out again while we looked at the framed pictures of her children set out on end tables. She was quiet for a long time, calculating the cards, their directions, and then she told Lucy their meaning. "You'll never find love," she said slowly, deliberately, as if she were a surgeon coming out to tell the family the bad news. "You'll never have children and you'll always be alone."

I couldn't understand it. Tarot readers don't tell you you're going to die in a car accident next Thursday. Wasn't a loveless life worse than that? Lucy walked out of the house without asking the question she was entitled to. I settled our bill. I should have said something to Jan, but what was there to say? Please take back the last five minutes?

I found Lucy sitting in the driveway next to a small inflatable swimming pool, crying. "Bullshit," I whispered in her ear and pulled her up to her feet.

I WAS TEACHING an undergraduate fiction workshop and babysitting five days a week for two of the poetry professors and coming up with just enough to scrape by. I know that I must have written a couple of stories that year, but all I remember is that when I wasn't worrying about money, I seemed to be over at Lucy's apartment, the two of us complaining about love. "Love and money," my mother said to me over the phone one night, "that's pretty much all anyone writes about anyway." No matter what the tarot reader said, I knew I had made a mistake almost as soon as I moved in with Dennis, and now I had to find a way to fix that mistake without the embarrassment of breaking up with him and moving again. In short, I had to make it work. Lucy's new apartment on Bowery Street had wood floors and high windows and a wraparound porch. It was more than what she could afford but she decided to go with it anyway. She got herself a couple of cats and an early-morning job at a bakery to supplement her teaching income. Living on her own, she had even more friends, more adventures, while my world narrowed considerably. After a year in Iowa City, Lucy had the same kind of fame she'd had at Sarah Lawrence. Everywhere she went, people knew her. It was always amazing to walk down a street with her, everyone waving as if she were gliding past on a rose-covered float. People stopped and wanted to talk to her. When she got on the bus, it was, "How are you doing today, Lucy?"

"How do you know everyone?" I said after the fifth person had called her name. "I must be the most socially inadequate person in the world."

"I don't know any of these people," she said. "They know me. No one forgets my face."

And then, of course, I realized that Lucy had never disliked me in college. She simply had no idea who I was. People made an effort to find out the details of her life. They knew her story and mistook that for actually knowing her, exactly as I had done. So many people thought Lucy was rude because she made no effort to return all the familiarity that poured down on her. It had gotten to be too much at some point years before I met her, and now she simply let it go. We walked past a bank with a drive-up window. A teller sat alone in a little glass box and watched the world go past her. "Hello, Lucy!" she called into her microphone.

Lucy looked at her, sighed, and then looked back at me. "That's not even my bank," she said.

ONE DAY, in an attempt to take my mind off my romantic problems, Lucy took me horseback riding with a friend of hers named Sally. Sally might have been having trouble with her love life, too, and Lucy was always up in the air about hers. It was a good excuse to get away for the afternoon. I had grown up on a farm outside of Nashville where we had a couple of horses. Most of the riding I had done in my life had not involved saddles. We drove out to a stable and after talking to the manager there, Lucy picked out our horses. I knew from the stories about the years she spent working in a barn during adolescence that she was completely in her element, but I had never seen her ride before. The backup plan in life, if things didn't work out with writing, was to break and train ponies. "You can get a fortune for a well-trained pony," she said. When they brought Lucy a horse to ride, she pulled down the reins so that the horse's nose was touching her nose, then she slid her fingers up under his upper lip and scratched his gums furiously. It was like finding that magic spot on a dog's stomach that sends them into fits of leg-thumping ecstasy. The horse now belonged to Lucy, and she swung up top to ride.

In my first winter in Iowa I discovered that if you wrapped your scarf too high around your face, the condensation of your breath would crystallize on your eyelashes and freeze them together in the time it took to blink. By July it was clear that the summers were so desperately hot, there was nothing to do but stay as still as possible and pant. But I had also found that there was a very brief time in between the freezing and scorching when the whole place was beautiful, thick and green and spotted with wildflowers. The day we rode our horses was one of those days. Lucy was out front, taking us fast through the trees while we whooped and laughed and pretended our lives were free and full of possibility. She was a beautiful rider, no bigger than a lark perched high up on a horse's back. Whatever she did, we followed her. She was like Willie Shoemaker, but lovely, all blond hair and sunlight. If you really stopped and thought about it, it would have been impossible to understand how someone so tiny managed to dominate something so huge, to dominate not only the horse she was riding but the two that were following behind her as well. But when you saw it in action, there was no question that such things happened. In those woods in Iowa, Lucy ruled the horses. Lucy ruled the world.

"You're a maniac!" I screamed when we finally raced back to the barn. I fell into her, sweating, thrilled.

"You're the king of all horses!" Sally said.

We had been gone for two hours. Lucy bought a Coke from a machine and poured it over her hand, letting each of our horses lick off her fingers.

It was such a good trip that I went back the next week and brought Dennis. I asked for the same two horses Lucy and I had, but when we were saddled up, we couldn't make them leave the corral. We stood in our stirrups, duded out in jeans and boots, and tried to talk them into taking a single step forward. They wouldn't budge. Finally someone who worked at the stables got on a horse and led us a quarter mile down the trail, but once he turned back, our horses only dipped down their heads and began to mow the grass beneath them. No amount of pulling or digging of heels could persuade them that there were human beings on their backs. If I ever thought I knew a couple of things about horses, I could now see that I was completely deluding myself. These same animals who had been such a joy the week before when Lucy was at the head of the pack were now complete strangers to me. I may as well have been sitting on top of a refrigerator. When they had eaten their fill, they ambled back to the barn, where a young man took the reins and asked us if we'd had a nice time. Dennis was furious and insisted that they refund our money. But we had been gone for an hour, and it wasn't their responsibility if we didn't know how to ride.

LUCY LOOKED FANTASTIC in those days. She spent an inordinate amount of time at the gym and was trying to eat a better diet. Eating was so difficult for her that the victory was never good food, but any food at all. Often all she managed to choke down were a couple of chocolate creams and half a doughnut. Now she'd discovered the weight lifters' secret of protein shakes and powdered vitamins that could all be thrown into a blender. She clipped down the streets in short skirts and perilous heels and took every catcall from a carload of frat boys as a badge of honor. The problem was her face. The last surgery she'd had in college seemed to be going the way of all the others. It was melting back into nothing. Due to the extensive radiation treatments Lucy received as a child, the reconstructive surgeries never seemed to last. If that problem wasn't devastating enough, she was facing an impossible insurance morass. She couldn't have another surgery done in New York, where she was no longer a resident. The alternative was then to do it at the University of Iowa Medical Center, where the doctor proposed a traditional pedestal surgery. Lucy would spend six weeks with her wrist sewn to her stomach to establish blood supply for a tissue graft. Then she would spend six weeks with her wrist sewn to her face while the graft grew onto the side of her jaw.

I was constantly forgetting that Lucy had a set of problems that were different from everyone else's, or that her suffering extended beyond the usual limitations of love and money. She didn't like her boyfriend, she was lonely, she was broke, she had a crush on a guy who only wanted to be her friend. Maybe her complaints were slightly louder, slightly more enduring, but they were basically the complaints of every woman I knew. And then she was there in my living room, pale and breathless, saying it again and again because neither of us could completely understand. "They want to sew my hand onto my face," she said.

"To hell with that," I said, and got up to get us both a drink.

*I got home from the hospital today to find my Saint Lucy medal waiting for me: I have always wanted one of those. Thanks pet: it's just so amazing to me how good you can make me feel, more than anyone else (sounds like a pop song, I know.)*

*My eye is still swollen, not so bad as Friday, but it's still a real problem aesthetic wise. Monday Mr. Fenton came round and said there wasn't really anything he could do, that I was stuck with this problem, that maybe it would get better, maybe it wouldn't, and in the mean time I had to decide did I want any more surgeries as that would surely make it worse. He was so flippant about it; short and curt, as if he were telling me anything other than this has been a total flop. It really upset me, what he had to tell me and the way he told me. I spent the night crying uncontrollably, all the nurses trying to console me. Finally, the head nursing sister came and talked to me and she said she'd let him know how upset I was. The next day he was supposed to come talk to me, but in the end he didn't have time, so now I'm supposed to go back on Monday. I just don't know, Ann, I just don't know. Sometimes I feel real calm and wise and accepting and other times I'm totally on edge. When I*

*wear the guise of alienated poet I do okay; everything seems if not actu-*
*ally good, then at least placable. When I try and wear the guise of a*
*woman, it's a disaster.*

Lucy used to say she was like a piece of modern art: "I'm finished when I say I'm finished." But at this point she wasn't anywhere close to being done. She could turn down the pedestal, but she couldn't turn down surgery in general for much longer. Her face was sinking, which meant, among other things, it was getting harder for her to swallow her food. She would just have to wait until she got out of Iowa before she could go back for another round.

WE TYPED UP our theses with the proper margins and they were bound and sent to the library to sit on the shelves with the theses of all the other writers who had graduated with a master of fine arts degree. The Writers' Workshop had been nothing but a wonderful stall, a place to go for two years when we had no idea what to do after college, and now that it was over, we were utterly adrift. I published a few stories at *Seventeen* and kept on babysitting. Lucy had her job at the bakery. I felt considerably less certain of my place in the world than I had upon leaving high school.

In the winter of 1987, I left Lucy for the second time. Dennis believed all our problems were in Iowa, and that once we left, we would be fine. Lucy stayed on in her Bowery Street apartment. I came to say good-bye.

"If I'm still here in a year, you'll come back and get me, won't you?" she said.

"With a gun, if I have to." I gave her the contents of our refrigerator and pantry and hugged her. I knew I was making another mistake, trying to justify the series of mistakes I had already made, but at this point I felt like I was on a train shooting off into the future. Once I was on board, we just kept going faster and faster and I could no longer imagine jumping off. Lucy was still my closest friend, but I couldn't help but feel like I was abandoning her as I got in the U-Haul with Dennis and drove back down the interstate I'd come by.

LUCY STAYED IN Iowa City until June of 1988 and then went to teach in a summer writing program for high school students and have another surgery in New York. After that she went to Berlin to live with a college friend whom she adored. It was too far away for her to come back for my wedding. I stayed in Nashville, worked at a bookstore, and got married in June of 1988 at the age of twenty-four. That fall, Dennis and I got teaching jobs at a little college in Pennsylvania. Things didn't get worse after we got married. I simply lost my ability to bear it, which in truth was never so good in the first place. On the last day of August 1989, I got a ride to the airport and flew back to Nashville a week before I was to start teaching for my second year. In the larger scheme of catastrophes, this one was probably not so enormous. We didn't have children, money, or property. We didn't even have a dog. But being twenty-five, Catholic, and divorced was completely devastating. I called my mother from the Nashville airport and for the first time told her I was having some problems.

I was an unemployed college teacher taking up residence in my mother's guest room. It was too late to apply for adjunct jobs at other schools, and I was in no shape to stand up in front of a classroom anyway. I started looking for work as a waitress, but I couldn't get hired. My resumé included a master's degree and several publications, including a short story in the *Paris Review*. By the fifth restaurant I figured it out. I gave myself a year of junior college and seven years of solid food-serving experience, operating on the correct assumption that no one ever checks references anyway. I was remade at a TGI Friday's, where I wore a short black skirt and a white pillbox hat with a net veil. Funny hats were a requirement of the job. Without a hat or a bunch of flowers or a record pinned onto your head, you were sent home from work. It reminded me of going to mass with my grandfather when I was a little girl, and how he would drop his handkerchief on my head if I had forgotten my hat. During a morning shift meeting in my first week of work, the general manager stood up to make an announcement.

"Today I would like to make a special presentation to an extraordinarily promising trainee. In the history of this branch of the restaurant, she is the first person to make a perfect score on her waiter's examination. Ann Patchett, will you come forward so that I may present you with the Wow pin."

The staff cheered and stamped while he pinned the tiny medal to my collar. It was true, I had studied. I knew the contents of every drink, the expediting procedure for every entrée. It had never occurred to me I'd be better off throwing the test.

"I want the pin," Lucy said when I called her that night.

"You want to wear my Wow pin?"

"We'll be pinned, my pet."


THE YEAR I TAUGHT in Pennsylvania I was extremely unhappy, but I had pulled it together every morning and gone to work. Aside from my office-mate, Diane, who offered me a lifesaving level of friendship and support, no one had any idea there was a problem in my house. Academia is no place to wear your heart on your sleeve. At Friday's, though, everyone knew your problems. One waiter was so behind on his child support that he was barely keeping himself out of jail. A cook who called me Little House on the Prairie in honor of my blond braid and notable lack of eyeliner, did go to jail, but only for possession, and we all went to visit him when we could. Regina, my best friend at the restaurant, was a smart black girl who wore a leopard-skin hat and liked to say that one day the management would make a big mistake where she was concerned and from then on out the chain would be known as "Regina's." She once called me at five o'clock in the morning for an immediate ride to the airport. She was in trouble, she said, big trouble, and she needed to go to Houston. I drove her there, covered her shifts, and then picked her up three days later, but she never told me what had happened. It was not the kind of friendship I was used to, but it was the kind I needed at that time. I traveled with the transient dishwashers, the all-powerful bartenders. We cried in the kitchen. I ran another girl's cheeseburger out to a table for her when she could not pull herself together. We kittied our money on hot summer nights and rented cheap motel rooms for the use of the swimming pool. We went to other restaurants after our shifts were over, drank margaritas, and tipped outrageously. We could afford to be generous because we knew this moment would not last. Every single person there believed that he or she was just passing through. We were all going to be something big, something important. I believed it about myself as well. I came back to my mother's house in the middle of the night and stood in a hot shower until I felt the grease and cigarette smoke run out of my hair, down my back, and into the drain. Then I sat on the bed and counted out my tip money.

Lucy had hoped to stay in Berlin, but she didn't speak German and her plans to teach English never materialized. When she was out of money, she went to London to live with her sister, Suellen, and

Suellen's husband, Joel. There she signed on for a temporary secretarial service, first typing reports for a private investigator, then briefly making photocopies at Gillette. Her new plan was to teach English in Italy, though later that switched to Japan and then Prague.

Lucy's plans for teaching and travel were put on hold when Suellen read an article in a magazine about a surgeon named Mr. Fenton who was doing revolutionary reconstructive work in Aberdeen. Lucy balked at the idea of going to see another unfamiliar doctor with a miracle cure, but Suellen had written to him and she thought his work sounded extremely promising. To seal the deal, she bought Lucy a train ticket to Aberdeen so that she could meet him. Mr. Fenton explained his plan for a tissue expander and a vascularized bone graft. He thought the whole process would take six months. Knowing that one is always better off doubling any amount of time projected by a plastic surgeon, Lucy figured she would be gone a year. In the end, the cycle of surgeries took nearly three years.

What surgery meant to Lucy and what it meant to almost anyone else were two different things entirely. For Lucy, a single surgery was more like a fitting for a dress, or the rearranging of living room furniture: it was only a step towards something else. She never gave up believing that there would be a final moment, a last surgery, a point at which her "real life" would begin. The damage that was done to her at ten would finally be made considerably better, if not right. Men would fall in love with her, no one would look twice, unless it was to admire. She would be freed from the greatest burden of her life. If that was the reward, then the pain and inconvenience of more surgery was not an unconscionable price to pay. Also, Lucy was a good patient. She understood the politics and dynamics of hospitals. She could be remarkably sweet and easygoing with an IV tube hanging off either arm. She loved to be told that she was the most difficult case they had ever seen. Of course she was. She was the girl from the medical books. She was the case study.

Enduring surgery, however, was nothing compared to enduring Scotland. Aberdeen was largely a rig town, which meant that many people worked on offshore oil rigs for several weeks at a stretch and came back fat with cash, looking to stay as drunk as possible until they had to go out again. It was a brutal place for tissue expanders. Lucy had her first one in the hospital. They placed a balloon under her skin and injected it with small amounts of saline solution over the course of about six weeks, giving the skin a chance to stretch out slowly to be used in a future surgery. Lucy, whose face was usually faulted for being too small, now had something that looked like a tire hanging off the side of her head where her jaw should have been. She stayed in the hospital, reading and talking with other patients, not having a particularly bad time. But after the surgeries progressed, it was decided that more skin, and thus a second expander, was needed. This time, instead of keeping her in, they sent Lucy home and told her to report back every day for her injection.

*Nothing seems to be working out for me, and I'm still wracking my brains to figure out where I went wrong. I am very negative about ever getting any sort of luck in writing or in love or anything at all. It's not just luck, I know I have to make things happen, but in the end you can't force someone to publish your work, or accept your love. Why I feel so negative I can't say, but I can't seem to make it go away. Every day I feel just a bit closer to the edge.*

*This balloon in my face is definitely not helping. I have managed to stay out of the hospital, but I have to go there most mornings. I get so self conscious around people that by the time I return I have a terrible*

*pain in my shoulders, neck and head. It will be at least another month
before the bone graft.*

One night after work I was sitting on the edge of my mother's bed,
reading her Lucy's letter.

"Save all of those," she told me when I was finished.

"I save some of them," I said, but she and I both knew I never was
much on saving anything.

My mother said it again. I was to save them all. "Someday you'll
both be famous writers," she said. "And these letters will be very
important to you."

## Chapter Five

This might sound a bit odd to you, but remember how Jan the tarot card reader in Iowa told you you and Dennis would always be together: when you two broke up there was part of me that was happy she was so wrong, because she also told me that I'd never meet anyone long term, never have kids (not that I particularly want kids, but the other part is sort of a harsh thing to hear from a fortune teller). What she said haunted me for a long time, but now I feel much better about it. (I'm sure you're not taking this the wrong way). The I Ching has been very unresponsive of late. It's like that sometimes, but then when you least expect it, it comes in right on the mark.

Well, my little lamp on the wharf, I'll end here. Please write, please give my love, to your mother, and please please please know that you are my most loved hero now and for always. Lucy.

Lucy and I wrote each other constantly and much of my tip money went into phone calls to Scotland. More than her face or even her love life, Lucy worried about her work. She was absolutely committed to the idea that writing would be her salvation and that she was obligated to pull herself out of all her present miseries with the sheer strength of her will and talent. Although she was still writing poetry, she was also working on a novel that was modeled after Nabokov's *Secret Life of*

*Sebastian Knight.* It was a story about going to search for an elusive brother, a theme that she came back to again when she tried to write a novel at the end of her life.

We both approached writing much the same way we approached going to the gym in those days: with the belief that regular attendance was more than half the battle. Lucy knew that she could write a novel if she just kept showing up and getting in a few pages a day. She told herself that Scotland could be the ultimate writer's colony, with financial support and limitless free time. On one side of her was an enormous well of depression waiting to be given over to, the voice in her head that said she was unloved and therefore unlovable, and on the other side was a daily page minimum and the copy of *War and Peace* she was reading, the belief that work would be her salvation and that the life of the mind would set her free.

On this point Lucy and I were completely united. We had written in college and graduate school and had our small successes, but we were writing to impress our friends, our teachers, possibly ourselves. Now writing meant something else entirely. Without writing, Lucy was just another patient in the surgical ward, waiting for her tissue expander to fill with the saline and stretch out her skin. Without writing, I was another waitress like all the other waitresses in Nashville who were waiting for their big publishing deal. They wrote songs. I wanted to write a novel. I was starting to see it was all pretty much the same thing. Lucy and I had ceased to be distinguishable from everyone else and every day the ground was getting softer, swallowing us up a little bit more. We had each come to realize that no one was going to save our lives, and that if we wanted to save them ourselves, we only had one skill that afforded us any hope at all. Writing is a job, a talent, but it's also the place to go in your head. It is the imaginary friend you drink your tea with in the afternoon. In her hospital bed or in her lonesome room back at her flat, Lucy brought out the sentences she knew and twisted them into poems and chapters, the same way I stood in the kitchen every night at the end of my shift at Friday's and rolled 150 silverware packets, dreaming up characters with problems more beautiful and insurmountable than my own.

Lucy applied for every fellowship, grant, and contest available. She pursued every possible venue for the publication of her poetry manuscript. She worked on her novel and had written a screenplay that an agent thought was promising. She applied for teaching jobs, artists' colonies, and sent out endless hopeful batches of poems to literary magazines. Everything went with a self-addressed stamped envelope for replies. I sent her books of American stamps and she used my mother's house as her return address. She didn't want people to think that she was living in Scotland and might not be available to claim whichever award should come to her. The process of putting the thing you value most in the world out for the assessment of strangers is a confidence-shaking business even in the best of times. But in Lucy's circumstances it was sheer heroism, a real sign of her devotion to her art. She was, in a sense, sitting at a craps table with her last stack of chips, trying again and again to hit it big. Rejections came in the form of polite letters, and everything she had dreamed might save her life vanished as soon as the envelope was opened. It did mean that I was the bearer of a lot of bad news, as I was the one who opened all the envelopes and then wrote to tell her.

*Dear ann,*

*This is the second letter I've written in the last hour to you. I had to tear the last one up because it's basic premise was how meaningless life was. I'm hoping this one will be a little cheerier, but also I guess it'd be dishonest to try and convince you that everything was hunky dory. I* *hate it here. I hate my flat, I hate my flatmates, I hate my writing, and most of all I hate myself at this moment. I have just finished consuming three doughnuts, which also makes me hate my thighs and my will power. I hate max garland* [because he had just won the Wisconsin poetry fellowship] *and I hate B——* and I hate Bush and I hate people who step on your toes in the street and I hate women with baby buggies and I hate Scottish weather and I hate kathleen turner because of her legs and the fact that she has sex scenes with michael douglas and I hate television and I hate p-town and the american poetry review and I even hate david foster wallace for being such a wally for complaining about being unmotivated when he's got two books published. . . . and I hate all the stupid men here who are short and I hate the fact that all of the above people don't even give enough of a damn to hate me. So much for the cheery letter, I guess.*

*What sparked this tirade is your letter today (not your letter, sweeties, but I mean the bad news that was in it). Four fucking times they've said no, get lost. And what ever made me think I could write a novel? What a piece of trash it is. And as for my poetry, well p-town's* [the Fine Arts Work Center in Provincetown] *told me in no uncertain terms what that's worth. Oh oh, maybe I'd better tear up this letter too. But then it'll take a week to reach you, and more than likely things will be different by then. Hopefully, this too shall pass. I just feel so baseless, rootless, but externally and internally. I think to myself, well, okay, do some writing, that'll make you feel better, but it's not that I can't write, I can actually sit down (I don't believe in writer's block) but that I hate what I write. Really: I'm not just saying that so people will counteract it, say nice things to me. Maybe I should stop thinking I'm some sort of artist and look at the actual facts of my never having really and truly succeeded at anything. Sure I was a star at college, but how many stories do we know of people who were stars at college only to do absolutely noth-*

*ing with the rest of their lives? All this surgery business is only delaying the inevitable while sending out some sort of smoke screen that lets people believe I'm doing something brave and strong (ha). The highlight of my day is watching Neighbours.*

In November of 1989, a month before I turned twenty-six, my step-father bought me a plane ticket to Aberdeen, knowing that time with Lucy was the best chance I had for getting back on my feet. It will go down in my personal history as the nicest gift anyone has ever given me. I took two weeks off from the restaurant and I was gone.

All through the flight from London to Aberdeen I stared out the window at the rough patchwork of landscape and thought how beautiful it was, how beautiful it would be to live so far away from my mistakes. It was a small plane and we did a good deal of pitching and tossing, but everyone got a nice cheese plate and a glass of red wine and I managed to hold my snack steady. The world that existed in the air over England and Scotland seemed extremely civilized, even sophisticated, and for those moments I thought that Lucy was leading a glamorous life, at least when you compared it to being a waitress in Tennessee.

SHE WAS CRYING when I came through the gate. She told me later she had come hours early to sit in the airport and wait for me. No one but Lucy ever cried because they were happy to see me, or cried from happiness just at the thought that I would come. When I saw her I had to make sure I didn't register any surprise. I hadn't understood about the tissue expander, even though she had explained it to me over the phone. I hadn't understood about any of it. Lucy's face was huge; the wide band of extra skin that sat on her neck was pale and fat with fluid. It was as

big around as her calf. She was crying and crying and I picked her up in
my arms and she wrapped her legs around my waist and we stood there
at the arrival gate for a long time, crying together.

On the bus back into town Lucy kept her arms around my neck, her
face against my shoulder, while I kissed the top of her head repeatedly.
She did not acknowledge the gawkers, who were brazen in a way the
Iowans never dreamed of being. No matter how aggressively I stared
them down, they simply held my eye.

"I'm so glad you're here," she said. She said it over and over again.

EVEN IF LUCY could barely remember the first four years of her childhood, she was still an Irish citizen and carried a large green passport.
Back in the world of socialized medicine she was for the first time free
of endless insurance forms, justifications, and debt. She also received
free rent and a reasonable stipend to keep her going while she had her
surgeries. She was living at the time in a desolate modern building that
reminded me of a YWCA. Every suite had a kitchen, a living room, and
six tiny bedrooms with a shared bath on a straight hall. Lucy's room
had a twin bed pushed up against the window, which looked down on
the street. She'd fixed postcards to the walls with pushpins and kept
her books lined up along the baseboard. She had a narrow dresser, a
tiny desk, and a twelve-inch color television that she rented by the
month. An extra cot was brought up from the basement for my visit
and when we unfolded it, we could barely open the door. We had to
walk across it to get to her bed. The whole room became a giant float-
ing mattress.

"It kinda makes you think how good we really had it back on Governor Street," Lucy said.

"Not to mention how nice the dorm rooms were in college."

"Oh," she said. "This is the state penitentiary compared to college."

The other girls who lived on the hall seemed years younger than we were. They wore heavy makeup and high heels to their jobs in shops, and while everyone was polite, each girl tried hard to pretend it was her flat and all these other people were merely passing through. Everyone wrote her name on her milk bottle and put it in her own section of the refrigerator. I had filled my suitcase with boxes of Cream of Wheat and jars of soy mayonnaise, two staples of Lucy-food that Lucy couldn't find in Scotland. We unloaded the goods into the third shelf of the cupboard, which was hers.

The November days in Aberdeen were short enough to be an afterthought of night, a poorly executed attempt at sunlight. Nearly every building was made from the plentiful Scottish limestone, so that even the most beautiful structures looked vaguely like prisons. The streets, the walls, the buildings, the sky, everything in Aberdeen was gray. We watched the weather reports on the news with rapt fascination. "They've got eighteen ways to say it's going to rain." Lucy got out of bed to act out the forecast along with the weatherman, sweeping her arms in wide circles over an imaginary map. "Watch for afternoon showers followed by a light mist in the early evening," she said in a perky voice. "Then there will be a heavy downpour with intermittent sprinkles."

Sad-looking women pushed their baby carriages through the crowds, the carriages covered in clear plastic sheeting that turned every pram into a little oxygen tent. In the morning we went to the Nile, a large, open restaurant that played nothing but Enya. All the waitresses greeted Lucy by name, but that was no surprise. We made our coffee last for hours while men in kilts trudged down the street in one joyless parade after another. I have never seen so much rain or so many parades. After the Nile we took the bus to the Royal Infirmary, where Lucy would have her tissue expander checked and filled with the day's injection of saline. I could see why she was happier there than she was in her flat. The building was huge and rambling with tiled hallways and a soft orangish light. Despite the size, it felt old-fashioned and strangely homey. Everyone at the hospital was glad to see Lucy. When she introduced me to the nurses, they seemed to be delighted to see me as well. "Ann!" they said. "We've loved your letters!" Lucy brought in all her mail to share, even the letters that came while she wasn't in the hospital.

After we finished up at the Royal Infirmary, we had just enough time to make it home to see *Neighbours,* an Australian soap opera starring Kylie Minogue that the whole city was enslaved to. The streets emptied out when *Neighbours* was on. It was completely spellbinding because, unlike America soap operas with their split-personality amnesiacs, this program showed a world in which nothing happened at all, a world not unlike Aberdeen. In the two weeks I was there a character brought a guest into the boardinghouse where she lived and the guest spilled a little nail polish on the living room carpet, where she had absolutely no business painting her nails in the first place. That drop of polish reached the level of Greek tragedy. Men discussed it in the pubs. Lucy and I talked about it for years.

It was dark by four o'clock and the rain would clump together to form a wet, heavy snow. Lucy and I would go to the gym and jump around in an aerobics class. The room was so packed that the wooden floor had an enormous bounce to it and I always ended the class feeling seasick. Lucy worked diligently to stay in shape. She wanted to bulk up, get some substance, but she was forever getting knocked off her routine by surgery. As soon as she felt she was as strong as all the other girls, she would be out again for six weeks.

At the end of the day we'd always wind up at Café Drummond, buy a pack of Silk Cuts, and tuck in for the night. Lucy would lean forward and take hold of my wrist. "Tell me the absolute honest truth." She stretched back her head as much as she could, which wasn't much. "How does it look?"

"How does it look right now?"

"Right now."

It looked like two loaves worth of unbaked bread dough hanging from the bottom of her face, but without the shine. I told her that it looked pretty bad. "But it isn't going to stay like this for long."

"Does it look like I have a balloon in my face?"

I studied her carefully, wanting to come up with another answer, then I told her, sadly, that it did.

Lucy nodded and sighed. "I know," she said. "I know."

As a child Lucy had been terrorized in the stairwells of her junior high and high school and had suffered relentless teasing and sundry cruelties about her appearance. But once she got to college, that pretty much stopped. People would gawk, but they weren't aggressive. No one ever bothered her in Berlin. But in London, little things kept happening: schoolboys followed her, calling her names; a man would make a face when he passed her. By the time she got to Aberdeen, it was junior high all over again. Children chased her from a bus stop. A handsome young man came up to her in broad daylight to say that his friend over there wanted to ask her out on a date while the friend screamed, "No, stop!" Packs of drunks would howl and bark at her as she walked home at night. Once, after she had gotten an apartment by herself, she had called me to say that she had run out of food and was too afraid to go to the grocery store because she was so relentlessly taunted. She was hungry. How does anyone on that day decide that instead of eating they will read fifty pages of a book on the history of French cinema, or write four pages of a novel, or type up a cover letter for a poetry competition that will almost certainly be lost? How does anyone pull themselves up over and over again?

Coming home late from Drummond arm in arm, a pack of laughing, stumbling men swayed towards us in the darkness, a half dozen
voices arguing drunkenly, each one trying to raise itself above the others. We were on a bridge, and though we automatically pressed close to
the railing, they were coming straight at us, like a car that crosses over
the center line to barrel its headlights into yours. They wouldn't have
let any two girls pass without a bit of friendly hassling. But when they
actually saw us in the intermittent pools of light, the thick fog of beer
they lived in lifted for a minute and we thrilled them. They barked and
screamed to be helped, rescued, saved. "Save me from the dog girl,"
they cried. It wasn't the first time it had happened since I'd been there,
but it was the time I had had enough. I let go of Lucy's arm and ran into
them screaming, smacking, shoving blindly into all there was to hate,
which gave them the biggest laugh of all. One of them grabbed me by
the shoulders and touched his nose to mine. "Boo!" he said. Dying of
laughter now, they tripped away while I screamed after them, "Assholes! Fucking assholes!"

Lucy came over and took my arm again and we walked home, both
of us looking straight ahead, neither of us saying a word.

That night I couldn't sleep. Everything in the world seemed cruel
and the taunting voices of drunks stayed in my head like a bad song. I
had a cough and at two in the morning I went to sit in the little living
room so I wouldn't wake Lucy. Usually one of the girls from the flat
was there smoking and making out with her boyfriend, but on this
night I was lucky and everything was dark. I turned on the little electric
heater and the television and curled up on the sofa, hacking. There had
been too much smoking, too much drizzly rain, and it had all caught
up with me. All I wanted was to be entertained, to think of nothing.
There on Scottish TV in the dead of night was Allan Gurganus, talking
about the publication of his first novel, *Oldest Living Confederate*

*Widow Tells All.* Allan had been my most important teacher in college. He was the person who had taught me to write. Now he was there in the living room in Aberdeen, handsome in his bow tie, calmly discussing his life as a writer. I was exhausted and running a fever. By the orange coiled light of the electric heater I felt like I was having a visitation from the Angel of Fiction. I decided then and there that I would be like Lucy. I would be like Allan. I vowed that I would write my way into another life. I, too, would try for everything.

TWO NIGHTS BEFORE my plane ticket said I had to go home, I gathered up all the one-pound coins we had and called my mother from a phone box. Lucy wanted to see if there had been any word from the latest round of fellowships she had applied to. Since I was gone, my mother, whom Lucy loved, was in charge of all her mail. What she told me was that she had come back from Alaska the night before. She had flown up for two nights on no notice because my sister had decided to get married.

"Heather's married?"

Lucy, tucked into the box with me, looked as surprised as I did. My sister had recently gotten a new job and left Tennessee for Alaska. I knew she had been dating someone, but married? "She wouldn't get married without me even knowing about it," I said.

"She's married," my mother said again.

I was divorced and now my sister was married and I had missed it completely. After I got a few details, her husband's name and what her name was now, Lucy took the phone and talked to my mother for the few minutes we had left. When she hung up, I looked at her, stunned. "I would have gone," I said.

"You don't have any money," she reminded me. "You never would have made it in time."

The whole business made me impossibly sad. I felt like my sister had just left on a slow trip around the world and I hadn't been at the dock to say good-bye. Shouldn't I have been there to wish her luck? Then again, what right did I have to be wishing anyone luck in marriage?

Lucy and I went back to Drummond for a drink. She started in on all our regular subjects: writing, how much longer the surgeries might take, how hard it was to find appropriate men when you have a tissue expander. I was having the conversation, but I was distracted, thinking about my sister married to someone I had never even seen a picture of. When we left the bar and started walking up the hill in the freezing damp wind, I was struck by the terrible mess I had made of my life. In the darkness I complained to Lucy: I was divorced, I'd quit my teaching job to get away from my husband, I was broke, and I felt impossibly far away from writing. I had missed my own sister's wedding.

"Oh, you'll be fine," she said lightly, wanting to move ahead to another topic.

I stopped walking, and after five steps or so she stopped too to find out where I'd gone. "I'll be fine?" I said. "That's it? I've wrecked my life, come to Scotland, and all you have to say is that I'll be fine?" I had spent plenty of time on her sadness and now I wanted a minute for my own.

Lucy came back to me and smiled. She looped her arm through mine and pulled me forward into the cold night wind. "It's true," she said, leaning her head on my shoulder. "It's your blessing and your curse. You're always going to be fine."

## Chapter Six

THE DAY THAT I LEFT ABERDEEN WAS SUNNY AND bright, as if to show me such a thing were possible. Lucy and I took the bus to the airport and cried all the way through the wide rolling fields of green grass. The road leading out to the airport provided some of the prettiest views around. The same gray rock that had made up every ugly building in the city could now be seen in its natural habitat, poking up roughly in the landscape and wrapped tight in moss. It was nearly picturesque. Five minutes into the ride I started wondering if the place really was as bad as it seemed, but I knew it was actually worse. I had seen the boredom and the loneliness and I could not understand how I was leaving her there. So I could go home to waitressing? Our friendship was like our writing in some ways. It was the only thing that was interesting about our otherwise very dull lives. We were better off when we were together. Together we were a small society of ambition and high ideals. We were tender and patient and kind. We were not like the world at all.

We stopped at the airport gift shop and I bought a scarf in a red tartan with the money I had left. "Write to me all the time," she said as we walked to the gate, her head back on my shoulder.

"I always do."

"Write to me more often now. I'm going to miss you more."

And so I left her there, knowing she would take the bus back to town alone and go back to that little room and curl up in a ball on the bed. I thought, What she wouldn't give to go home to my mother's house and work at Friday's. There was nothing glamorous about the plane ride home. It was only exhausting, lonely, and long.

*Dearest Angora,*

*So I went to see Mr. Fenton this afternoon, and now here I lie on my bed—he decided to admit me after he saw how swollen I was. Take a few drugs, have a few x-rays, I'm into it. Who knows if I'll get better, but at least I have the feeling something is being done. Unfortunately it's a Friday, which means I have a very boring weekend ahead of me. At least during the week there is always some sort of flurry to watch, but weekends are deathly, if you'll excuse such a word being used in such close proximity to the word hospital (or infirmary, as the case may). I was going to bring my computer but it's absolutely pouring outside and I didn't want to risk it.*

*I had to stop writing for a short while as I sensed I was about to get terribly boring. Shouldn't I say something deep or something? I mean, I am supposed to be a poet, aren't I? One day I want to get a job as Poet in Residence, if only because I think it's such a hilarious title. The only better job title I can think of would be Triumph of the Human Spirit in Residence. You could have the Cruel Yet Compassionate Chair in Writing. Nothing wrong with being patronized, I say, just so long as you're well patronized.*

For the most part Lucy and I applied for the same things. The places offering fellowships and prizes had some for fiction and some for poetry, and even though Lucy was working on a novel, she only considered herself a poet in those days. In this way we could overlap without actually competing. It was our greatest dream that we would both get a spot at the Fine Arts Work Center in Provincetown and be together. The Fine Arts Work Center admitted ten writers and ten visual artists yearly for seven-month fellowships. You lived in housing they provided and they gave you just enough money to keep you going. I had applied for a similar though considerably more upscale program as well, the Bunting Fellowship at Radcliffe, something that Lucy wouldn't do until the following year. I had made the cut at the Bunting and now was in the top three finalists for the fiction position. I was all but packed and ready to go. Since I had quit my last teaching job a few days before classes began, I could hardly ask for references in order to get a new teaching job. I needed to prove myself in another way entirely if I was ever going to clear my name in academia.

The thought that I might be going to Radcliffe made me place the parsley sprig on the cheeseburger plate with a little more flair than I had before. I was working on a couple of short stories, but most of my time was spent dreaming up a novel about a woman who sought refuge in a home for unwed mothers in rural Kentucky. Each morning before the restaurant opened every member of the waitstaff took a number that assigned his or her cleaning task for the day. One draw was to climb a high ladder and wipe down the antiques and bric-a-brac that lined a perilous shelf near the ceiling, including lugging up a little handheld vacuum and sucking the dust off the vast collection of taxidermy that gave the restaurant its character. Because I seemed to be the only person who was afraid of neither heights nor dead animals, whoever drew that number would invariably ask to trade assignments with me. Day after day I could be found scooting along the crown molding, hoovering off the stuffed foxes and wolverines, all the time thinking about my characters, a group of lost girls waiting to have their babies at St. Elizabeth's. I polished up the foxes' bright glass eyes with the soft hem of my shirt and thought of Lucy. We were all better off living in the worlds inside our heads.

That afternoon during the lunch rush one of the other girls asked me to run two pans of fajitas out to a table for her. Fajitas are a mess. They sizzle and pop, inevitably leaving little pinprick burns on your arms, the smoke nearly blinding you by the time you reach your destination. I stuffed the two plastic flats of tortillas in my apron, picked up the two iron skillets with attached pot holders, and shot out to table 23, trying to move fast enough to leave the smoke behind me. "Who gets the chicken?" I said brightly.

Had it not been for the smoke I would have seen her in time to swerve back to the kitchen and have someone else bring out the food. It was Lisa Truly, the girl from my high school who had, in my memory, been named the most beautiful, most talented, and most likely to succeed. And to make it worse, we had been friends. It was the problem of leaving your hometown for New York, vowing never to return again and then returning under less than noble circumstances. I held up the heavy metal skillets. The smoke drifted and waned.

"Ann?" she said.

I said hello. Lisa seemed very glad to see me. To her credit, she did not seem to take into account that I was wearing a striped shirt and serving her food. "I heard you were teaching college," she said.

"I was."

She nodded, as if there was nothing particularly strange about the progression of my career path. "This is my fiancé, Jason," she said, and her tall and handsome man smiled. "Jason, this is Ann. I've told you about Ann."

"Sure," he said nicely. "You're the smart one."

Had I been, years ago? "Who gets the chicken?" I asked again. I felt like my arms were going to snap off.

*        *        *

I DID NOT GET the Bunting. Neither of us got the Wisconsin fellow-ship. Lucy got into an artist's colony called Yaddo for the summer but the surgeries were extended and in the end she had to turn the resi-dency down.

*Dearest Pet,*

*. . . it's late and I only just woke up. I have to be at the hospital in an hour, so once again I'm using this as an excuse not to write. I get so depressed I can't move, even getting out of bed this morning was only finally accomplished as I finally had to pee. I don't know how to deal with everything, it's just too much for me. No mail again either: I've been hoping Yaddo would write me back since I told them I couldn't go, but they haven't and I'm afraid I've blown my one chance to go have a nice time someplace to spend the summer with a balloon in my face. The new yorker sent me back my poems, which I expected, so now I've tried the paris review. At least I haven't stopped trying, and I also know that I will manage to get at least one page of fiction written today, which isn't the six I demand of myself, but at least it's something. It's a continual effort on my part not to feel like a failure. I have picked up again on my correspondence course on getting a TEFL diploma, though I doubt I'll get to use it any time soon. I've really got to go back to the states soon if I don't want to blow my green card, but it's so hard to know when all the surgery will be over. I'm so afraid that I'll have to have another soft tissue graft. What the hell, I can't even think about it: that would keep me here until god knows when, not to mention how horrible those sorts of grafts are anyway.*

*Am I complaining too much? It must get sort of boring for you. I've got these three cats staying with me who are really over the top. They're*

*nice and sweet during the day, but at night: werewolves. Up the curtains,*
*in the cupboards, in the garbage, everywhere. I come in in the morning*
*and it's like a bomb hit the place, so I've taken to locking them away in*
*the hallway at night. They're good company though. . . .*

  *I got a letter back from the film place I sent my screenplay saying*
*they didn't want it but thought it was well written and showed a lot of*
*talent, and if I wanted to I could send in other stuff and it would get a*
*priority reading. I don't have another screenplay to send though, proba-*
*bly won't for some time, but at least it's some encouragement. For the*
*first time in my life I've found myself praying for actual things; before I*
*only prayed for stuff like wisdom and love and states of mind. These*
*past few months though I've been much more materialistic. I want defi-*
*nite action on God's part. Is this wrong? I worry that I'll get punished*
*somehow. I need to get out of this mess, but I just don't know how, so I*
*ask for his help.*

  *Well, I'll go now. Take care, write, give yourself a bear hug for me.*

I read Lucy's letters sitting on the edge of the bed in the guest room,
still wearing my uniform, smelling of French fries and beer. My feet
hurt up to my thighs. I was starting to wonder if I was ready to be a
writer, not someone who won prizes, got published, and was given the
time and space to work, but someone who wrote as a course of life.
Maybe writing wouldn't have any rewards. Maybe the salvation I
would gain through work would only be emotional and intellectual.
Wouldn't that be enough, to be a waitress who found an hour or two
hidden in every day to write? If Lucy was struggling to find her way
under the burdens of surgery, surely I could find it in the comfort of my
mother's guest room. I made my resolve to work for the love of the
work, to write for myself, but it didn't have to last for long. My luck
took a magnificent change of course. I was awarded a seven-month fel-

lowship to the Fine Arts Work Center in Provincetown. I had, in short, been saved.

I had to tell Lucy I was going to Cape Cod without her, our best dream of going together now lost in the wake of my good fortune.

She screamed. She cheered. "That's brilliant!"

"Really? You aren't upset?"

"How could I be upset?" she said. "It's perfect. Now you can go cozy up to the poetry judges and seduce them into voting for my application next year."

I was flattered that she thought I had the ability to seduce anyone into anything.

That summer I took every shift I could get. In the high-turnover world of food service, I now had enough seniority to work Friday and Saturday nights and Sunday brunch. I counted up thick rolls of greasy dollar bills and recorded the amount on a piece of yellow legal paper I kept at the bottom of my money box. I was once again the ant, putting away every dime for the long cold winter ahead. I scratched my orders on a pad and kept my eyes fixed on the novel I would write. I had until this point only written short stories but now I abandoned them for good. I saw those seven months in Provincetown as my big chance and I felt the need to do something big. I needed to change my fate, and the way I saw it, that was simply asking too much from a little story. Fate like mine would need an entire novel to be reordered and fortunately I had one in mind.

I packed everything I owned into the trunk of my car and said my grateful good-byes to my mother, who had kept me for over a year without a single complaint. I took too many detours and stopped to make too many visits on the way up and so got to Provincetown on October 3, when everyone else had arrived on the first. I had missed all the introductions, the getting-to-know-you beach parties. I moved into my tiny apartment in the cluster of houses the Work Center owned, moved my bed into the kitchen/living room, and set up my desk in the closet-sized bedroom with the nice window. I unpacked my computer, plugged it in, and typed the words "Chapter One," because everything has to start somewhere. I began to write the story that had been my companion in the restaurant for the past year. It was all in my head and now all I had to do was figure out a way to get it down on paper.

For three days I found the work sustaining, but the fact that I knew no one, really no one, was beginning to overwhelm me. One night well after dark I was talking to a friend in New York, complaining of loneliness. He told me to hang up the phone, go outside, and start knocking on doors. When someone answered, I was to ask him or her, depending on the door, if they would be interested in having a drink with me.

"Are you kidding?"

"Think of it as an assignment."

I looked out the window. It had already been dark for hours. "It's too late," I said. "I'll try in the morning."

"It's nine o'clock. Artists don't go to bed at nine o'clock," he said, and hung up the phone.

I had spent a lot of my life trying to find quiet time alone, but I had very little experience with being lonely. Now in the starry darkness of the Cape Cod night it was that loneliness that drove me to follow directions. The fellows at the Work Center are housed in a group of buildings that make a circle around a parking lot. I knew my downstairs neighbor wasn't home because the floor that separated us was so thin I could usually hear him breathing. I sucked up my courage and knocked on the first door I came to, but no one answered. I didn't have any better luck the second time. Lucy would have banged on every door. She would have led all twenty writers and visual artists down

Commercial Street in a conga line to the Governor Bradford and talked the bartender into buying every last one of them a drink. I rallied myself to try again. This time a porch light flicked on and the door opened up. A woman with pale skin, dark hair, and perfectly applied red lipstick stepped outside. I introduced myself, explained my situation, and asked her if she wanted to go for a drive. Elizabeth McCracken and I wound up at the Ben & Jerry's in Wellfleet, having a conversation that would be the start of the next great friendship of my life. It was the best piece of luck I'd had in years.

BY THE TIME Lucy came to visit in December, I had a set routine of reading, writing, and editing with Elizabeth, I had started dating one of the other fellows, a fiction writer named Eli Gottlieb, and I had finished the first hundred pages of my novel. My world was two miles long and a mile wide, I had no money, and I was completely happy. Lucy had come back to the States to ensure the continued good health of her green card and break out of the monotony of Aberdeen for a while. She wasn't finished with her surgeries, but she had been granted a temporary vacation from them. She came from a whirlwind of friends and parties in New York, planned to spend two weeks with me, and would then go and spend Christmas with her mother.

I'd like to say I re-created the moving welcome Lucy gave me when I arrived in Scotland, but she was planning on taking the bus up from New York and she wasn't sure which bus she'd be on, when it might arrive, or where it would drop her off. I gave her good directions and told her I'd leave the door unlocked in case for any reason I missed her.

But I was there after all. I heard her bags hit the floor and she yelled, "Pet!" When she bounded up the stairs to my apartment, she was an entirely different version of herself, with a new face to go along with

the new outlook. Gone was the tissue expander, the hugeness, and
while she was still swollen from a recent surgery, I could for the first
time imagine where all of this was going. There was something that
was shaping up to look like a jaw. She screamed in pure joy and leaped
up into my arms. She was her full and passionate American self again.
She was in Provincetown, after all, where even in the winter a handful
of six-foot-three-inch drag queens still ruled the streets, their stilettos
hitting the pavement like hammers onto nails. No one looked twice at
a girl with some lumps on her face when they could instead watch the
rose parade of men float by in their dreamy feather boas and dog col-
lars. Lucy was invisible, exuberant, and utterly birdlike in her wild,
darting freedom.

"You look amazing," she said. "Did I tell you that?" She threw off
her jacket, a sweater.

"Me? *You* look amazing. Lucy, your face is really shaping up."

"Do you think?" she said, and touched her chin lightly.

"It's all been worth it."

"I'll wear it to the party then. We've been invited to a party."

"A party?"

"Some guy I met on the bus coming up. It should be fun, a little
dancing. When's the last time you went dancing?" She kicked off her
boots and struggled out of her jeans. "Can I try your sweater on? I like
the color."

I pulled my sweater over my head and handed it to her. "Whenever
I saw you last was the last time I went dancing." I picked her sweater
up off the floor and put it on. It was tighter than mine, dark green, very
sexy, not entirely clean.

She took my sweater off again and handed it back to me. She was
down to her underpants and disappeared inside my closet, looking to

make herself over. She was sick of trying to wrap her scarf in the right way, sick of trying to cover up, hunch down, be small. She was interested in being as large as possible now. She pulled my stretchy black cocktail dress over her head at noon. Gone were our insular days in Aberdeen when there was no place to be but together. Lucy put her leather jacket back on and then her boots. I had to say, it worked. "Is it terrible if I go out for a minute? I ran into Marie on the way here. She wanted to know if I could have lunch."

"Not terrible at all." I was happy to see her so happy and anyway, I still had pages left to write.

She kissed me hello and good-bye and went out to knock on every door she could find. There was no trace of the morbid duo we had made up in Aberdeen. We were free.

Provincetown is nearly a ghost town in the winter, the faintest outline of its booming summer self. There weren't many people around but Lucy wanted to know all of them. She made plans to exchange work with the poets and have studio visits with all the visual artists and meet everyone for drinks and a game of pool later on. Because I was never any good after ten o'clock, she made her late-night plans with strangers. All she had wanted was to get into Provincetown and now she was exactly that: in.

I was a little concerned about how Lucy would respond to Elizabeth and Eli, but she was in complete approval of my choices and went on to have great friendships with both of them, especially Eli. Lucy and Eli were a lot alike, something I had never realized until I saw them together. They were both extremely smart, serious readers, great conversationalists, who wanted more than anything to leave their desks and find a party. They each had countless friends from every period of their lives and they liked to brag about their connections. If I wanted to find Lucy during her visit, the first place I went looking was Eli's, where more often than not they were sprawled on his giant sofa, telling stories and making each other laugh hysterically.

As much as Lucy liked my friends, it was important for her to know at every moment that she was my uncontested favorite. There was nothing subtle in her methodology. When we had lunch with Elizabeth, Lucy would inevitably leave her chair at some point during the meal and come and sit in my lap.

"What are you doing in my lap, pet?" I asked her.

Lucy would lean her head against my chest and turn her eyes up to me. "Do you love me?" she said.

"Of course I love you."

"Best?"

"Yes best, but you are crushing my thigh."

Lucy sighed, contented now, and continued her conversation with Elizabeth from the comfortable vantage point of my lap, eating what she could off my plate.

I was a little embarrassed, but only because I was afraid that Elizabeth might not understand Lucy, or understand me for letting her get away with it. I was used to Lucy's behavior, but when I had the chance to see it from the fresh eyes of a stranger, it looked fairly questionable.

In my furnished apartment there was a funny little foam-rubber chair that folded out into the narrow bed that Lucy slept on in my study, or some nights I slept there and she slept in my twin bed in the kitchen, but in the morning we were always in one bed or the other together, drinking coffee and talking. Now that she was here, Lucy was certain of her destiny: she would go back to Aberdeen for the briefest time and lay down the law with her surgeon, Mr. Fenton, to whom she had become quite close. They would get this business of her face finished up once and for all and then life, real life, would begin. Lucy had felt she had been on the verge of real life several times before, a life with the finished face she would have to learn to live with, but it had never quite happened. There was always one more surgery that was holding her back. This time it was going to be different. It was going to be true. She would win a fellowship to Provincetown, she would have a dazzling life as a writer. She would have friends and fall in love and go dancing every night.

Having Lucy in my apartment those weeks was not unlike having a couple of those revved-up cats from the Scottish Cat Protection League. She ran all over the place, left my clothes tossed over lampshades, wet towels heaped under pillows, bowls of Cream of Wheat minus three bites in whatever spot I was most likely to step in them. She came home in the middle of the night wanting to talk or show me some impossibly sexy way the gorgeous gay men were dancing in the club she'd just come from. She made a blood-chilling number of long-distance phone calls whenever I was in the shower and insisted on sitting in my lap whenever I tried to talk to someone else. I, on the other hand, was writing my novel as if it were a factory job. It was already late December and by the first of May the fellowship would be over. I had figured out exactly what I had to do every week in order to finish on time, because after May 1 I didn't have one clue in the world what was going to become of me. All I wanted to do was work. Fortunately for both of us, Lucy found plenty of people to play with.

Our plan was to leave the Work Center on the same day. I would go home to Nashville for Christmas and she would go on to her mother's in western Massachusetts, but when the time came, there were too many invitations to good Christmas parties and so Lucy put her mother off for a few more days and stayed in Provincetown without me. She ate from my plates and wore my clothes and slept in my bed like Goldilocks while the benevolent, lumbering bear went south for the holidays.

WHEN I CAME BACK after Christmas, there was nothing but work. Michael Klein, the poet who lived downstairs from me and had, of course, become great friends with Lucy, was known to open my door and shout up the stairs, "Stop typing so much!" as my computer sat right above his bed and the sound of the clicking keys drove him crazy after a while. I walked on the beach in the morning in the freezing wind and rain, cultivating a kind of insanity wherein people who do not actually exist start talking to you. For the first time in my life, I thought about dying and thought that it would be an awful thing, to step accidentally off a curb and into a speeding car, because if I were to go I would take the entire cast with me. Half a manuscript for a first novel that has no author to finish it is always thrown away. The thought of all of them lost panicked me in a way that thoughts of my own death never had before. I had come to believe in these people, and they deserved their ending. Every chapter I finished I took to Elizabeth, who marked it up for me and gave me a short story in return, which I marked up for her.

Then finally one day everything I had imagined for these characters while I was at Friday's was down on paper. I wrote the last sentence of *The Patron Saint of Liars* in early April and stumbled out of my apartment and into the beautiful spring feeling panicked and amazed. There is no single experience in my life as a writer to match that moment, the blue of the sky and the breeze drifting in from the bay. I had done the thing I had always wanted to do: I had written a book, all the way to the end. Even if proved to be terrible, it was mine. I found Elizabeth and we both printed out our books and stood on them to see how much taller they had made us. Then we went down to the Governor Bradford to celebrate the day.

LUCY HAD GONE back to her life in Aberdeen after the New Year, but this time there was an ending, a light. The surgeries, which could have gone on more or less forever, would finish up in June. Yaddo had granted her the month of August for the second year in a row and this time she was going to take it. She was turned down again for a fellowship at the Fine Arts Work Center, but before she even had the chance to feel badly about it, her good luck rounded the corner like a racehorse and she was awarded a Bunting Fellowship at Radcliffe. She would start just after Yaddo. She would have an office, a community of fellows, a stipend of $23,000, full privileges at Harvard, and no responsibilities other than to give one reading. If one could think that there was any order in life, then Lucy was about to step out of the darkness. She was going to be rewarded for her years of valiant effort.

I finished the final revisions for my novel at the end of April and on the first of May said good-bye to dear Elizabeth and Eli and drove my book to New York. I cried all the way to the Sagamore Bridge. I had once again made all the usual rounds of applications—Wisconsin, Bunting, Exeter—but hadn't wound up with anything for the next year. I was planning on going back to Nashville and resuming my life as a waitress. I was completely out of money. When I got to the city, I went first to *Seventeen,* where I had published a few stories and articles. My editor there, Adrian LeBlanc, had become a friend and said she would let me use the enormous Xerox machines in the office to make copies of my book. Adrian and I were both twenty-seven. She spent her days at *Seventeen* and her nights in the South Bronx writing stories for the *Village Voice* about teenage prostitutes and drug dealers. Once I was there in the mecca of fruit-flavored Lip Smackers, I realized the last fifteen pages of my book had somehow gotten lost in transit, though it still seems impossible that such a thing could happen. I sat in Adrian's office and typed them up from memory on her IBM Selectric. I had signed with an agent years before, after publishing a story in the *Paris Review* when I was twenty-one, so when I'd finished up at *Seventeen,* I drove the whole thing over to her office, dropped it off, and turned the car south again to Tennessee.

I took an extra day to drive in big loops around the Shenandoah Valley. It was the midway point between where I had been and where I was going and it was beautiful, placid cows and long grass in the shadow of mountains. I thought as long as I was there, both parts of the trip would stay suspended: Provincetown wasn't really over; I wasn't headed home again.

When I finally gave in and turned to Nashville, I got there quickly. My mother met me in the driveway and threw her arms around my neck as if I were a soldier come home from the wars. She wanted to know where I had been, what could have taken me so long. She told me to call Lisa Bankoff, my agent. In the time it had taken me to drive home, the book had miraculously sold. I called Elizabeth and Lucy first to tell them the news because what good is news without girlfriends? They were thrilled.

*Dear Angora,*

*I've received many hand written letters from you (this in response to the opening line of your last letter).*

*I got out of the hospital yesterday and look like I've had a good right cross to the chin and lip. I had some fat from my hip grafted into my lower lip, so now I've got what will hopefully be a bridget bardot lip,*

*though it's doubtful it will last more than a few months, meaning I'll
have to decide then if I want to do it again. It makes a difference: I can
close my mouth now and can kiss, which I find very exciting. It was sort
of nostalgic, having my very last operation on old ward 39 (did I tell you
Mr. Fenton is moving down south this September?). I think now I can
honestly say that I am happy with the way I look and will only be having
maybe a few minor operations from here on in; providing of course that
nothing terrible happens. I still need lower teeth, but that will come in a
few months time. My eye is still bothering me, but I've got a new cam-
ouflage coiffure and hide it behind my bangs. Everyday I have to fight
the urge to cut all my hair off, but that's another story. I've been writing
a page a day of an autobiographical story, but other than that it's zilch.*

Lucy came back to the States in late July to start her residency at
Yaddo. She had given up on her novel and was back to poetry full-
time. I went to Kentucky in the fall, where, with my new book contract, I had landed a last-minute job teaching literature and fiction
writing, filling in temporarily for someone who had taken an unexpected leave of absence. Lucy and I both had a place to be, and we had
won that place on the strength of our work. I believed there had never
been such luck in all the world.

## Chapter Seven

FOR MUCH OF HER LIFE LUCY WAS ABLE TO USE THE historical atrocities of humankind to keep her own despair in perspective and, therefore, slightly more manageable. She decided to make herself a student of suffering, but it had to be the right kind of suffering to capture her imagination. She wasn't interested in forces of nature. Towns wiped out by hurricanes and earthquakes were useless for her purposes. People buried under rubble were sad, but they offered her no strength. She was sensitive to hunger; because of the difficulty she had with eating, she was often hungry herself, but it had to be a famine brought on by war and not a simple lack of rain. She wasn't particularly moved by illness either; in fact, at times she could get a bit competitive on the subject. "People talk about having chemotherapy," she said. "They don't even know what chemotherapy *is*." What she meant was back in the days when she went in for treatment, they burned you alive. Now that the whole business was so civilized by comparison, she thought it only fair that they should come up with another name for it altogether. Lucy assessed the pain of the body by the standards of her own experience and found that just about everyone else came up short, especially those on whom the ravages of illness could not be seen. She once became terribly jealous of a beautiful woman who had ovarian cancer because to Lucy the disease had done nothing but increase the woman's glamour. "I wish I had ovarian cancer," she said sullenly.

Where Lucy found her courage and camaraderie was in persecution, the kind of systematic cruelty where absolutely nothing is left to chance. Stories in which people are destroyed because someone else chose to destroy them were the ones that lit a fire under her. She read the chapters of Butler's *Lives of the Saints* as bedtime stories. In her heart she climbed onto Catherine wheels and crucifixes with her heroes. She loved Christ for His suffering, for what they had in common. With all His strength, even Christ had asked if this burden could be lifted from Him. The idea that pain was not a random thing but a punishment of the evil upon the good, the powerful upon the weak, gave her something to rage against. After all, what is the point of being angry at nature when nature could care less? If you cried against barbarism, then at least you were standing up to a consciousness that could, hypothetically, be shaped.

When Lucy believed that there were actually things in the world that were worse than what had happened to her, she could pull herself up on this knowledge like a rope. When she lost sight of it, she sank.

*I'm about to finish Primo Levi's Auschwitz book. I don't know if I discussed this with you on the phone, but rereading it now is an intense experience for me because of my relationship to that book as a child. I was so miserable then and all around me were people complaining about their lives, and I would look at them and wonder how they could be so ungrateful, if only I had what they had, etc., etc. I'm not sure how I was able to turn this around to myself, but one day I realized maybe my accusations of ingratitude could be pointed at me. That was when I became obsessed with the Holocaust, with the Vietnam War, and the*

*various famines going on then. I would walk around for days pretending*
*I was in a concentration camp, or that I was going to trip a landmine at*
*any moment. I know it sounds morbid, but it helped me enormously:*
*everything, everything seemed suddenly important to me. I think those*
*years really shaped me, possibly even began poetry for me. Now, reread-*
*ing Levi's book has reminded me of myself. I'm a different person now;*
*possibly in the way Levi was a different person when he was older. It*
*scares me a little: Levi did kill himself after all, but it interests me greatly*
*precisely because I am at a total loss to describe how I am different, how*
*what I know now differs from what I knew then. This is a language*
*problem: the disparity between the two selves, between the two sets of*
*truths, is very real and clear to me, yet my ability to control this knowl-*
*edge in any sort of narrative or verbal way veers off constantly. Like the*
*dreams where you suddenly realize you don't speak the language, or*
*the other dreams of driving some car, some wonderful car but when you*
*sit behind the wheel you have no idea where you are. Maybe it's self-*
*obsessive, but I'm quite fascinated by it. It's stirred me into thinking that*
*maybe it is time to start something non-fiction about it all. Right now*
*I'm almost finished with a semi-autobiographical short story: I'll see*
*how I feel about it when I get through that.*

When I read *Survival in Auschwitz*, I tried to imagine a girl sick
with radiation and chemotherapy, as bald as anyone in a concentration
camp, probably as thin. I imagined Lucy balancing the weight of such
epic suffering on her shoulders in order to press her own suffering
down. It isn't possible to use the death of six million to make oneself
feel lucky, because after a while the enormity of that pain simply
replaces your own, making it different and in no way better. "It is lucky
that it is not windy today," Levi writes. "Strange, how in some way

one always has the impression of being fortunate, how some chance happening, perhaps infinitesimal, stops us crossing the threshold of despair and allows us to live. It is raining, but it is not windy."

*Dear Ann,*

*An important thing happened to me a few days ago in Prague, though I haven't yet reached a point in time at which I can know how it was important. The background begins several months ago, when I bought a book of very contemporary American and German paintings. There were a lot of names (painter's names) in the book I recognized, having tangentially heard them over the past few years, Fischel, Clemente, Schnabel, Basquait, but with whose work I wasn't actually acquainted. I've always had a hard time with so many contemporary painters - I've never been able to be really moved by the work - it always seems somehow exclusionary & even snobbish to me. But I liked this book: looking at the paintings in it I felt for the first time that maybe there is something to all these new points after all. Basquiat's (and I'm spelling his name from memory, I may have it totally wrong) work, however, I didn't like, and even felt a strong aversion to. His paintings consist mostly of thin line drawings of a number of small objects, scribbled onto a background of paint. The objects he draws vary from scrawled tables to jawbones, and often there is indecipherable writing accompanying them, sometimes achieving the effect of some kind of diagram and/or uninterpretable instructions. There's usually a very disturbed, manic quality to them. But as I said, the paintings never worked for me—I want to say they seemed posed, but perhaps I'm only reaching that conclusion in retrospect. But to continue; several weeks ago I happened by chance, perhaps only because the title was in English, to pick up a book of drawings in a bookstore here in Berlin. They were exactly the same as his paintings, only without the paint: the same frantically drawn thin lines, the same bizarrely juxtaposed subjects. To my great surprise I found that I liked them as drawings. Really liked them. Mostly, though, I liked them in retrospect: they were the sort of things that changed with memory, and the more I thought about them in my head the more valuable they became to me. And of course they were no longer in front of me: I didn't really have much desire to return to them physically again and again and again, which somehow came to be the point for me, that they were intensely mental acts, not physical. Added to this (though I used to think this ("this" = the history of any artist's life) shouldn't matter: now, after what's happened, I have to rethink this) is the content of Basquiat's life: he died of a heroin overdose at the age of twenty something a few years ago. I felt very affected by the drawings, and moreover, I felt very excited by my excitement itself: I'm such a cynic most of the time and here, for the first time, I felt genuinely affected and moved by work that had seemed impervious to me earlier: I felt as if I'd made some sort of breakthrough. Then last week I was in Prague. It's a stupendously beautiful city, but it was packed w/ tourists & just as I was walking around thinking it was all a bit too much like Disneyland, I came across a museum in the old Jewish Ghetto which housed the drawings of Terezin. Terezin was a children's concentration camp, and the drawings were done by children there, while they were there. The first floor (it's a very small place) houses pictures of the children's memories & hopes for the future: six year old's versions of dogs and giant flowers and school and landscapes where the sky is a thick blue line at the top of the page. Apart from the occasional appearance of a jewish star on a coat or armband, they could have been done by any children, and it's the viewer's knowledge of what became of the children which makes them almost unendurably heartbreaking. I was very moved & upset by them, but I kept my composure & went to the second floor. There, I found drawings about the more immediate surroundings of the children. A nine year old's version of a beating by a man with a club & a swastika. A hanging, drawn exactly as we used to draw the word-game of "hangman" when we were children. A long line of people, circles for heads, triangle bodies for the women, waiting on a long line at the end of which is a rectangle shaped figure with a dog drawn as circles, and beyond that two tall thin rectangles with curls of smoke coming out of them. I started to cry, and even now as I write this, remembering them, I have to keep stopping and trying to compose myself, as I'm writing this in a public place. The most terrible of them all was still to come though: it was very very simply drawn, the child couldn't have been much more than 7 or 8. First on the left was just a sort of free-floating head, rather comically and ineptly drawn: a sort of rectangle with a funny blob for a nose. Next to that was another head, lower down, obviously a cartoon version of a fishbone: they were the person's ribs. And standing over that was another figure, the head drawn like this:* 😟 *, and then another awful terrible body of ribs. It had arms also, and one bone in the arm was drawn much differently than the rest of the drawing: very carefully, and heavier: the drawer obviously spent most of his or her time on this detail, and I could even imagine they were proud of it. It was a bone, drawn in cartoon-understanding of armbones:* 🦴 *. The rest of the arm was only a scrawl, and you could just barely see it was holding a sickle, or scythe:* ∧ *. It was a child's version of death. I am never ever ever going to get that drawing out of my head. But there was something else about the drawing too: the oddness, the carelessness w/one careful but random detail sticking out - it was exactly the sort of drawing Basquiat would do. I was so shattered by the drawing that I felt an extreme amount of anger at Basquiat: he seemed like such a fraud to me. And more than that, I felt thrown back into my previous distaste & dislike for most contemporary art, but worse, because in my previous distaste I had my cynicism, which is rarely more than a* *symptom of inflated ego anyway, to keep me company. Now—it's not even dislike I feel, I could deal w/that because it would be a polemic which would, by its very existence, mean that there was an alternate state of acceptance & "like". Now I don't even have that: I feel so empty about art right now—I feel it is a genuine crisis. I haven't lost hope though. In fact, I feel that once I have worked my way through this that I will know something I didn't know before. But what? And why should I think it will be of any value to me? I'm going to have to digest this for a long time.*

*Later the same day now, which also happens to be my birthday. 28. Ugh. How did this happen? No matter how aware I try to be of time's passing, it just seems to slip away. I remember the first time I ever got the idea that perhaps poets were interesting people was in high school english, reading Our Town; the bit about how only poets are able to really sense the passing of time.*

*I have been musing some more about what I've said in this letter. My whole concept of art has taken a serious shaking, and I am beginning to see what I can get from this, which has something to do with a better understanding of. . . . christ, I don't know. I did know for a minute there, but then I had a coughing fit and now I've forgotten. That is one thing I've learned, that it is possible to really understand things at certain points, and not be able to retain them, to be in utter confusion just a short while later. I used to think that once you really knew a thing, its truth would shine on forever. Now it's pretty obvious to me that more often than not the batteries fade, and sometimes what you knew even goes out with a bang when you try and call on it, just like a lightbulb cracking off when you throw the switch.*

*It is a beautiful day, I bought myself a fruit torte and three chocolate truffles to celebrate my age oldness. Soon I will finish this letter and go and sit in the sun and read the paper and eat my truffles. Life really is pretty good most of the time, so long as I remember to keep looking at it that way. I got a letter from Shelia which bummed me out a little about a certain romantic prospect I had in mind: he's living with someone else now. I have also heard through the grapevine that Miriam Kuznets will be at yaddo this August as well (she is the one sigman was seeing), so maybe I will be able to find out, hopefully, what happened to him. I'll be back in the states so soon—it frightens me a bit. I've even bought luggage and everything. I will call you the very first thing when I fly in. I called my twin sister to wish her a happy birthday and she said she and "Bob" will pick me up at the airport. I've never met "Bob," yet I always have this strange compulsion to put his name in quotation marks.*

*Love and all that razzmatazz*

*Lucy.*

## Chapter Eight

WHEN I WAS YOUNG AND DECIDED TO BE A WRITER, my understanding of the job description came straight from *La Bohème*. There would be a drafty garret, cold nights, little food, a single candle. On the upside, I, like Puccini, imagined the garret would be in Paris, which would give the poverty a glamorous edge. When Lucy left Aberdeen in 1991, she left a true garret, one that was isolated, depressing, and utterly bereft of singing bohemians. From there she stepped into that other truth about the writer's life, the one we had heard so many rumors about: The Gravy Train. For writers looking for care, feeding, and companionship, there are a myriad of options, and after all our countless applications we had finally cracked the code. We were in, and in the years to come we would systematically work our way through just about every perk that was available to us. Lucy was spending her late summer at Yaddo, where I had spent August two summers before. Yaddo is a capital *M* Mansion in Saratoga Springs, New York, complete with Tiffany windows, elaborately carved banisters, formal gardens lined with white pillars, fountains, and a pool. There are trails to walk in the woods and rules that say if you pass someone during the day you may simply drop your gaze to the path as a signal you are thinking seriously about your work and do not wish to engage in conversation. Nor is your creative process disturbed by household tasks: your sheets are changed and towels arrive in big, fluffy stacks. Breakfast and dinner are taken in the enormous formal dining room, but lunch comes in a pail to be eaten in your study or by the pool, depending on the weather. It was a world so far away from tissue expanders and hospitals that it's hard to imagine a plane could get you from one place to the other. It seemed that there should have been a decompression tank, some sort of halfway house to live in for a month that was moderately nice so a person could come up slowly to avoid getting the bends. The bends in this case were a sort of eight-year-old giddiness that made one want to run up and down the red-carpeted stairs late at night, banging on every door on every floor, wanting to look and see who had the best bedroom.

*Dearest Pet,*

*It's raining here today, the first time since I've been here. Finally yesterday I got a brand new poem going, but today it's harder to keep up with it. I'm amazed, though, how conducive this place is to working. I think I was really afraid of the idea of being locked away, but it's just the opposite. The fact I know I only have a month is motivating too, yet at the same time, since each day seems like a week, it isn't frightening either.*

*Last night Miriam Kuznets (Sigman's ex) and I went for a walk around the grounds, that dirt road which takes you past the lakes. I guess I don't have to go on and on about how wonderful it is here, as you already know. The only thing missing is you, but I'm sure we'll be here together if not next year, then the year after. I guess they don't let people in over and over, year after year, but I take a lot of comfort in knowing that, unless something really drastic happens, I'll get to return again; it relieves me of that awful oh-my-god-I've-got-to-cram-it-all-in-right-now feeling.*

*I lost a dollar playing poker last night. About six of us played, and Tom was the only male. I hate men when they know they're the only one, but Tom seems fairly oblivious to it. He seems like a very laid back kinda guy. Michael Ryan is here; he on the other hand is perfectly aware of his status as male. He's a really nice man, but something about him. . . . or maybe I'm just jealous, because he seems to flirt with everyone except me. I'm having all the same ego and self-esteem problems that I've always had, but I think I'm doing a good job in not letting it interfere with my work. I've decided I'm going to go get into some kind of therapy when I get to boston. Last night, or rather the night before, a whole group of people were sitting around talking about how therapy "saved their lives"; it was all a bit hokey, but hey. It's become sort of the regular thing here to go to the Adelphi bar each night at ten forty-five, as reward for working from after dinner until then. There aren't any drinkers here, not the ones of yore anyway. In fact, I seem to drink the most out of anyone.*

Before the days of cellphones, receiving a call at Yaddo was a big event. There were two pay phones in the hallway leading into the din-ing room and while you could call out anytime you liked, incoming calls could only be received during the dinner hour. Getting a call through was not unlike dialing in for a radio contest. Some nights I would punch in the number for a straight hour and get nothing but a busy signal. (Was it better to keep dialing the same line? Did switching back and forth increase your odds?) You had to hit it exactly, the moment someone set the receiver into the cradle, because everyone who knew anyone in that dining room was dialing just as frantically as you were. Ah, but when it rang, I could see it all so clearly in my mind. I knew that some skinny poet dressed in black jeans would have to get up from his dinner and go down the hall to answer. He takes his time, ten rings even though it was busy ten seconds ago. (People who had just hung up the phone never wanted to pick it up again.) "Yaddo," he barks, or if he is very clever, he says, "Pay phone." I would ask him politely, "May I speak to Lucy Grealy?" And with that he drops the phone with the full force of his disappointment that it is not, in fact, for him. I listen while the receiver bangs against the wall. He returns again to the dining room and for a second everyone looks up, hopeful, perhaps, that the call will be for them. "Lucy," he would say, "it's for you." She pushes back her chair and rises into the pool of evening light coming in from the leaded windows. Somewhere, someone behind her mutters, "It's always for Lucy."

I called every night. I wanted to talk to Lucy and Lucy wanted to be the kind of person who got the most calls. The phone booths were unbearable, hot and narrow as upright coffins, so we never talked for very long, but it meant that when she went back to her seat, everyone would look up again and someone would ask and she could give a little lopsided smile and shrug. "Just a friend," she'd say mysteriously.

What she told me was that she was depressed because she'd made a pass at Tom, who rebuffed her and then made a pass fifteen minutes later, right in front of her, at a pretty girl who had already received three passes that night. Yaddo was summer camp the way summer camp is represented in movies, with intrigues and crushes and sex. A few nights later Lucy told me that her friendship with an older painter was taking an interesting turn. He adored her and paid his undivided attention to her in the evenings when everyone sat on the back patio to smoke cigarettes and watch the bats dive for mosquitoes. He held her in his arms and talked about Russian literature. He pointed out the sparrows from the bats. Then he started taking Lucy to bed. The cuddling had progressed to different variations of kissing and nibbling and touching. But no actual sex.

I wanted to know why in the hell no actual sex?

"He has a girlfriend." Lucy sighed. "And he has to be faithful to her because he's a good person. He has to be true to her and true to himself."

"Oh, for Christ's sake."

"Maybe he'll change his mind. Maybe he'll fall in love with me."

"For three more weeks? Why put yourself through the heartbreak? This is not a good person, Lucy. Good people don't do this sort of thing."

"He is good," she said. "Call me back tomorrow and I'll tell you what happened."

"Shouldn't you eat dinner every once in a while?"

"Most of the time I can't eat what they have and even when I can eat what's offered, I'm usually too intent on not slobbering it all down my chin and lap that I barely get anything into me. I think one or two of the women here suspect I'm anorexic or something."

"So try and eat. No one is going to care."

"I get frozen yogurt in town," she promised.

So every night I called and got the new installment on the non-affair. They progressed to sleeping chastely naked in one another's arms. Then on the first of September he left summer camp, happy in the knowledge that he had never cheated on his girlfriend. And Lucy was left to cry over him for six months.


WHILE OUR PLAN was always to land the same fellowship at the same time, it never worked out that way. We won the same things but our good luck was always slightly out of sync. I was a finalist for the Bunting Fellowship at Radcliffe while she was on the waiting list at Provincetown. Two years after Lucy had her Bunting year, I had mine.

Two years after I was a fellow at the Fine Arts Work Center in Provincetown, Lucy got to go as well.

With her fellowship at the Bunting Institute, Lucy was given money to live on, an office to work in, and a group of extremely smart women to interact with, although she groused about the fact that they were always too busy working to go to the movies during the day. Lucy had spent enough time alone working in Aberdeen. What she wanted now were people to go out to lunch with. Her need to surround herself with friends was enormous, and she diligently tracked down everyone she ever knew who had landed in Boston. Her letters were full of notes on who she had tried to call so far that day and who had yet to return the call and what a good conversation she had had with someone else. In Scotland she had braced herself for loneliness which was, after all, as abundant as rain. There wasn't much she could do about it. But in Cambridge she didn't want to be alone for a minute. She decided to give up her apartment and find herself some roommates. She also decided to follow through on the decision she had made at Yaddo and sign on with a therapist.

*I had a very interesting time with that shrink yesterday. She can't see me for much longer, it's the way the system is set up, but she's going to try and find me someone who can see me on a regular basis. What was interesting about yesterday is that I had an actual insight, the sort they say you're supposed to have in therapy but of which I've always been a wee bit dubious. It wasn't an overwhelming insight, simply that although I was aware of it, I've never noted the significance of the fact that 90% of the men I've slept with, I've slept with almost immediately and then gone on to become friends with them, rather than allowing it to progress the other way. From this we got into the negative self-esteem thing and*

*she said this extraordinary thing: I can stop it. I don't have to feel so bad*
*about myself all the time. This struck me because I remember speaking*
*with Michael Ryan at Yaddo, he was telling me about his whole life*
*spent looking in the mirror and hating himself, and now he doesn't do*
*that any more. I was sort of flabbergasted in the way both he and the*
*woman yesterday just so categorically said Yeah, we can fix that. Like it*
*was an infection or a bad tooth or something. It was the objectifying of*
*it that startled me, and I'm attracted to it, to thinking it's something you*
*can change, though of course I don't believe it, yet that, according to*
*Michael and the shrink, is part of the problem, a bona fide symptom of*
*it. Curious, very curious.*

While Lucy was in Cambridge, returning phone calls and making
lunch dates, Patricia Foster, a friend from graduate school, asked Lucy
to write an essay for a book she was editing called *Minding the Body:*
*Women Writers on Body and Soul*. It was exactly the push she'd been
waiting for. Lucy took the semiautobiographical short story she'd been
working on and turned it into an autobiographical essay. Nonfiction
about herself. It was a piece about her cancer, pain, chemotherapy,
teasing and longing and shame. It was about the wonderful freedom of
Halloween masks and getting to walk around like any other kid in the
world for one night a year and the horrible oppression of a world full
of reflective surfaces. I read the manuscript sitting at my dining room
table in Murray, Kentucky, and felt like Lucy had just slipped a knife
into the ground and sliced open a diamond mine. The writing was
stunning, better than her best poems. Not only had she found her story,
she had found all the room that prose allows. Her life was no longer a
metaphor for something else. It was a narrative that was itself as powerful and magnetic as she was a person. After spending so much of her

youth trying to turn people's attention away from her face, she now
pulled the light directly onto her jaw, her childhood, her humiliation. It
was a decision that sent her in another direction entirely.

Since the essay was written for an anthology, Lucy had the chance to
place it in a magazine first. It was accepted by *Harper's,* Lucy's first
choice—we believed, in those days, anyone's first choice. The publication won her a National Magazine Award. Because the essay was so
clearly an overview of a complicated and compelling life, it also won
her an agent, who got her a book contract with Houghton Mifflin. Then
she finally won the fellowship to the Fine Arts Work Center in Provincetown she'd been trying to get for so long. The following year she'd have
someplace to go and write the book. Lucy Grealy had come to glory.

She was also furious with me. In November of 1991 I'd moved to
Murray, Kentucky, where I would be teaching for one semester starting
in January. The first night I was there, Mark Levine dropped by to
introduce himself while I was unpacking boxes. He taught poetry and
would have the office down the hall from mine. There wasn't a lot
going on in Murray. It was a dry county with a Wal-Mart, a Dairy
Queen, and one excellent doughnut shop. A new girl in the English
department was a fairly big event for other members of the English
department. Mark had gone to Iowa after I did and while we had never
met before, we knew a lot of the same people. He stayed for hours, sitting on the floor and talking to me while I unloaded books into a bookshelf. It wasn't too long after that I was dating a poet.

"No," Lucy said.

"I'm not asking permission."

"You can't date a poet."

Lucy had never met Mark, but she hated the very idea of him. He'd
won the prizes at Iowa that she had wanted but didn't get. He had been
a favorite of Jorie Graham, a powerful and brilliant poet whose

favoritism Lucy had greatly courted over the years but had only rarely received. Even if they hadn't overlapped in the program, even if it had all been years ago anyway, she saw him as direct competition. He had published poems in the *New Yorker,* and in her mind he had taken up the space on the page that was destined for her.

"Do you like his poetry better than mine?"

"Lucy, this is insanity! I've only just started going out with him."

"Do you think he's a better poet than I am?"

I was sitting at the top of the stairs in my new apartment and the lights were off. I leaned against the wall and tapped the receiver on my forehead. "I've only read a few of his poems."

"So you think he's better." She had made everything into a contest and there was no sense in me trying to tell her it was otherwise.

"Of course I don't think he's better. I think you're better."

"Do you love me more?"

"Of course I love you more, even though I believe it's perfectly possible to love more than one person and to love different people in different ways but if we're talking straight-on comparative love with no adjustments for circumstance then, yes, you win hands down. I love you more. In fact I don't even love him. I've only been going out with him for two weeks."

"I love you, too," she said, but she said it in a wretched voice.

Lucy called three or four times a day with the sole purpose of reminding me that while I was in the middle of nowhere Kentucky teaching four classes and being buried alive by student papers, I was ruining her life.

"I'm all alone," she would start.

Standing at the kitchen sink, I put down the potato and the peeler and braced myself to go again. "You're not all alone. You have a ton of friends in Cambridge. You go out every night."

"I don't have a boyfriend. Nobody loves me."

"For God's sake, Lucy, I love you. Everybody loves you."

"It isn't the same. You wouldn't understand."

I wouldn't understand because I was dating a poet and thus committing the ultimate act of betrayal. "Listen, pet, everything is going your way right now. You have a piece coming out in *Harper's,* you've got the greatest fellowship in the world, you're living in Cambridge. I'm living in rural Kentucky and teaching my ass off. Why am I the one trying to cheer you up?"

"You have a boyfriend. You have a book coming out."

"You have a book contract! You can't feel hurt because I have a book coming out. You're going to have a book coming out, too."

"I haven't written a word of it. It just hangs over my head. I spend my entire life feeling guilty that I'm not writing and I don't actually write anything at all. Your book is completely finished. You have nothing to worry about."

"So start writing," I said. "A page a day. You used to write every day in Aberdeen. It's not as if you've sold a book and you've never written before."

Then I could hear her tearing up over the phone. She sniffed and choked and the sadness was as real as anything. "Will I ever have sex again?" she said.

"Probably tonight," I said. "Probably before I will."

Two or three hours later she'd call back and we'd do the whole thing over again.

The fact is I had a great deal to be happy about in those days, but then so did Lucy. I couldn't understand how she could present so much misery to me when so many of the things she had dreamed about had come true for her: she was out of Scotland, her face was greatly improved, she had an important fellowship at Radcliffe and a book contract and a large circle of devoted friends. It was true, she didn't have a boyfriend, but that wasn't reason enough to overlook everything else. Of course it also occurred to me that Lucy might have been doing pretty well, but to allow me to think so would be letting me off the hook for my most egregious breach of our friendship: the poet.

In February I was going to New York to give a reading at Sarah Lawrence and I asked Lucy to drive down and meet me there. She grudgingly agreed. I thought it was possible that she could come and not speak to me at all, but I had to try.

In the course of most lifetimes, few people are capable of the kind of enormous changes that Lucy seemed to manage every year. Maybe this ability had its origins in her physical self, the constant state of transformation she went through even when she wasn't in the middle of a surgical cycle. But it wasn't just her face that always showed up different. I had known her shy and cool in college, scrappy and James Dean–tough in Iowa, then all decked out in high heels and tiny black cocktail dresses. She had been as sweet and loving as the best child one could possibly know and she had been wild as the worst kind of teenager. She worked constantly on deciding who she would be, her philosophy and approach to life. When I saw Lucy this time, she was right at the start of a whole new phase. She was just becoming famous. There was a light sheen of confidence sitting over her shoulders, the glow of someone whose attention was desired. She was driving a red Saab that she'd bought with her book advance and wearing an artfully distressed leather jacket. She was slightly harried and distracted, as if I had just called her out of a very important meeting. She was affectionate and distant and she made it perfectly clear that her feelings were still sore. She wasn't so sure that coming here was worth her time.

"Traffic," she said, and rolled her eyes to explain her late arrival.

I had spent the day on campus, teaching a couple of classes, giving a reading, seeing old teachers who had been so unfailingly kind to me. It was wonderful to be back, and now I was here with Lucy in this place where we had started off together. But we were awkward with one another as we walked around campus. The wind was freezing and reminiscing wasn't enough to sustain the evening.

Lucy suggested we go to the movies, and afterwards we would go to a nice restaurant, one of the ones we wouldn't have been able to afford when we were in school. I thought it was a waste to sit in silence in a dark theater when we only had one night together but if the alternative was walking around not saying what was on our minds, then I might as well take it. We drove the scant mile into downtown Bronxville and saw the film of the David Mamet play *Glengarry Glen Ross*.

They should have billed it as a horror movie. As the salesmen scraped and begged and lied to keep their lousy jobs, Lucy and I leaned in closer towards one another, the desperation of their lives closing up our throats. We held hands. When the supervisor berated them, we shut our eyes. By the time the lights came up, we were sweating and exhausted and had somehow been restored to ourselves again. We could talk. Even after we got to the restaurant and ordered two glasses of wine, we were still shaken up.

"My God," Lucy said. "What if we weren't writers? What if we had to work like that?"

"I wouldn't make it." The chances I would wind up in sales were about the same as my becoming a prize fighter.

"But what if we had kids? What if we had a husband to support? What if we were like them and we couldn't walk away?" Lucy pushed the heels of her hands against her eyes. "What if I never make it?"

"I think you already have."

"If I can write this book, maybe. If anybody wants to read this book once I write it."

"Of course people are going to want to read it, and as for writing it, I think you have to now. Otherwise you're going to owe Houghton Mifflin a lot of money." I thought of the red Saab. I had a strong suspicion it wasn't going back.

That night we slept in the house of a woman who rented out rooms to Sarah Lawrence visitors. It was the same room I had slept in more than ten years before when I had come up to see the college for the first time. Lucy and I tucked into our little twin beds and I clicked off the light between us.

"Don't be mad at me anymore," I said in the darkness.

She was quiet for a long time. "I don't like him," she said.

"You've never met him. Even if you had met him and you really didn't like him, which wouldn't happen, couldn't you just be happy for me because I'm happy?"

"I wish I was a poet."

"You are a poet. It's just that now you're something else, too. Now you're a soon-to-be-famous memoirist."

"That's a horrible word."

Neither of us said anything for a long time, and after a while I thought Lucy had fallen asleep. The curtains were old and thin and the light from a street lamp fell in through the window and showed up the small outline of Lucy in her bed. "Okay," she said finally.

"Okay what?"

"I won't be mad at you anymore."

## Chapter Nine

I HAVE NEVER IN MY LIFE KNOWN A WRITER WHO enjoyed the actual act of writing less than Lucy, which is saying something because just about every writer I know sits down to work with some degree of dread. When she started her fellowship at the Fine Arts Work Center in Provincetown in the fall of 1992, she was filled to the top with all good and serious intentions. She was going to write every day. She was going to go to the gym. She was going to lead a quiet life of reflection. Despite having written her *Harper's* essay, she felt she was leaving the Bunting Institute having frittered her year away (although in her defense I must say that everyone I have ever known who had a year at the Bunting, including myself, felt in the end that they had frittered it to one degree or another). All signs pointed towards success in Provincetown. First, she had the book contract and an absolute deadline and Lucy was someone who relied heavily on the pressure of deadlines to get anything done. John Skoyles, who had been Lucy's favorite poetry teacher at Sarah Lawrence, was now the director of the Fine Arts Work Center, and my friend Elizabeth had come back for a second-year fellowship, so Lucy had two friends before she even got there. She also met Joy Nolan, one of the fiction fellows, when she first arrived and Joy became one of the great friends and allies of her life.

To be in Provincetown in the winter is to be broke. Nearly all of the stores and restaurants closed and life is reduced to a skeleton crew. Most of the people who are left hole up to paint and write while the cold wind blasts down the suddenly empty Commercial Street. With her book advance in her back pocket, Lucy was, by the standards of those around her, well-to-do. She chose not to stay in one of the houses owned by the Work Center, where the other fellows can easily chart a person's comings and goings. For an extra fifty dollars a month over what her fellowship provided, she rented an apartment in a tall, narrow wooden building that looked directly over the bay. The entire structure rocked and swayed with every storm that blew past. With her Saab and her good view of the water, her friends and her contract, Lucy was suddenly the one with the glamorous life.

But no matter how hard she tried to stay inside and write, the simple act of being alone was nearly impossible. Lucy could most often be found at the Governor Bradford, one of the only year-round bars, where she tried her hand at pool in the afternoons and talked about how hard it was to live under the pressure of pages owed. She bought her friends beers and punched in songs on the jukebox. At night she went dancing with Joy, favoring the clubs dominated by handsome gay men. Lucy loved dancing at gay bars. If she was ignored, there was an easy explanation for it. Besides, she was such a good dancer she was rarely ignored. Unlike Aberdeen, where it was so hard to get to know anyone, or Cambridge, where all the other Buntings were often busy, there were always people to hang out with during a Provincetown winter.

But with all the tourists gone and the beaches empty, there were no diversions except the ones you made yourself. Every alley, every house, every bartender, became completely known. The winter days at the end of Cape Cod were breathtakingly long, as if every hour had an extra fifty minutes squirreled away inside it. There were no responsibilities, no place you had to be. The only constant was a steady gray drizzle. Lucy and Joy were forever getting in the car and setting out in search of adventure, anything to make this minute feel in some way different from the one before and the one that was coming up next. Once on their way home from Wellfleet, they found a horse running loose in the middle of North Truro Center. After a good bit of effort, Lucy caught the horse and then, holding it by the halter, they walked it from house to house until they were able to return it to its owner. Lucy loved the story and she told it over and over again. "She was thrilled," Joy said, "because she got to be the hero *and* there was a horse."

This is not to say that the days were all bars and horses. Lucy was writing, but it came in short bursts and the bursts weren't coming often enough to bring her up to the number of pages she needed. In February she threw a "Congratulations, You've Wasted Half Your Fellowship" party and everyone came and danced in her apartment and had a wonderful time.

But more than the writing or the sameness of the days, what took up Lucy's time was love. She had fallen in love with another painter who was amicable and ambivalent. He was interested in Lucy, they had slept together a few times, but he wasn't sure what he wanted, and now he thought that maybe he would rather just be friends. I had seen Lucy brokenhearted over men before, but this was in a different category. It was, I think, the first time she had actually loved someone instead of just feeling hurt that someone had failed to love her. Whenever I talked to Lucy in Provincetown, she was crying.

"I'm ugly," she said.

"You aren't ugly."

"I'm ugly and I'm going to be alone for the rest of my life."

"Listen to me, pet. What you're going through is awful, it's really awful, but it isn't a judgment on your future. You aren't ugly and you aren't going to be alone forever just because things didn't work out with this guy."

On the other end of the line she would cry and cry and I would hold the phone and wait for her to come back to me. "I'm tired," she said finally. "I don't want to be alone anymore."

I was too far away to do anything more than listen. I had moved to Montana with Mark, where he had gotten a teaching job and I would later start to teach as well.

*The other night I dreamed you called me on the phone to tell me you weren't going to Montana, that you were coming to P-town after all. I was so happy, and the dream seemed so real that I spent half the morning thinking it was true.*

It wasn't like Aberdeen, I told myself. Lucy wasn't alone. She had Joy and Elizabeth. She had dozens of friends. She could walk into any coffee shop in town and find someone she knew who would sit down and talk to her, someone who would stroke her hair while she cried and then make her shake it off and go dancing at the A-House. But I had lived in Provincetown myself and I knew how long those winters could be.

By SPRING LUCY was still brokenhearted. Her fellowship was nearly over, and she had passed her deadline for a book that was nowhere close to finished. She extended her lease in order to stay on through the chaotic Provincetown summer, even though her rent skyrocketed to meet the exorbitant standards of the season. In the summer it was a different town altogether. It was as if the first warm day brought 100,000 people pouring in like locusts. The drag queens and Rollerbladers and lesbian bikers packed the narrow streets alongside the sunburned tourists pushing baby carriages. Every shop and restaurant and art gallery was open and stayed open half the night. In the Mardi Gras atmosphere of constant celebration, Lucy finally buckled down and blasted through the last hundred pages of her memoir. For the rest of her life she figured that this was the way she worked best, writing very little through most of the time that was allotted to her and then making a heroic eleventh-hour save. "That's the way I wrote my book," she would say, proof that the system worked.

And of course she was right, it did work, but being the ant, I never understood the pleasure of barely slipping something in under the wire. I had spent the winter out West, methodically chipping away at my second novel, stacking up the pages at my regular steady pace. Both of our books came in at about the same time, but Lucy's was forever accompanied by a story that made it seem breathless, lucky, magic, while mine was pretty much just a book.

Lucy loved having a story to tell. It wasn't enough to have written a brilliant book about surviving cancer and all of its ensuing brutality. Lucy absolutely insisted on the idea that she lived a charmed life, perhaps as a way of counterbalancing the parts of her story when charm had been in such short supply. She wanted always to believe that she was someone who simply fell into things, she was lucky, one of the blessed few who always found the right place at the right time. And because she insisted on it, it did in fact happen for her quite often, though never as often as she needed it to. She needed it to happen about once every eight minutes. For her thirtieth birthday (which she dreaded; she could not abide the business of aging) she went to Greece alone, took up with a fisherman, and they made love on his boat without a word of common language for her entire birthday. Proof, surely, that her life was charmed.

One of her favorite stories had to do with finding her apartment in New York. She had tried for an entire day to do it like everyone else, with the folded-up real estate section of the newspaper and the phone numbers of a couple of brokers, but she hated it. Pounding around the city from one overpriced, unglamorous place to the next was for losers, clowns. Exhausted and demoralized, she stopped into the Spring Street Bar in SoHo to have a drink for courage. The guy on the stool beside her was older and almost handsome in a broken-down, disheveled sort of way. He had paint on his hands, which meant he could have been an artist or a day laborer. Whoever he was, he was also looking for courage in the middle of the day. He took a sip of scotch and asked her how it was going. She told him in great detail.

He nodded. "I've got a place you could have," he said. "I've been meaning to rent it. I was going to put the ad in tomorrow. It's right next to mine. We could be neighbors."

Lucy didn't know if the guy really had an apartment or if he was just trying to pick her up, but if it was a pickup then that might not be such a bad way to polish off the rest of the afternoon. Lucy followed Stuart around the corner to Mercer Street, up two extremely long flights of stairs, and into the loft next to his, where she would live for the next five years. The apartment was perfect, but the story was even better.

I had also found a new apartment. It was about a third of the size of Lucy's and a fraction of its glamour too small to calculate. The floor was covered in a low-napped carpet that gave shelter to a kingdom of tiny, biting ants that no amount of extermination could dent. I had left Montana for Cambridge, having finally won the Bunting Fellowship I had come so close to in my waitressing days. Once Mark and I were living on opposite sides of the country, we fell apart fairly quickly, so now I was East Coast and poetless, which made Lucy extremely happy.

We could see each other every weekend or two, taking the train back and forth between Boston and New York. For the smallest crisis, I could be there in three hours. I had finished the novel I proposed to write during my fellowship a week before the fellowship started and I was at a complete loss as to what I should be doing with myself. Among the innumerable perks of the Bunting Institute is being able to audit any class and the right to eat in the faculty dining room, so I found myself taking courses in the history of architecture and having long, expensive lunches that were charged to my account. Every day I went to Blodgett Pool with a music historian who also had a fellowship. It was the single most regular thing in my life and I often thought as I day-dreamed away the laps that I had been given a prestigious fellowship in swimming.

Of course I'd drop everything to go to New York. What was there to drop?

SOMETIMES I WENT to see Lucy every week, but she wasn't the only thing that brought me to the city. Mark Levine had won a Whiting Award the year before and at the ceremony I met a man I had no memory of meeting. He wrote to me months later to say I had made a real impression on him and he had made it a point to read my novel, which he thought was something very special. By then I was in Boston and he wanted me to come to Manhattan so that he could take me to lunch at the Lotos Club and discuss my future. My future was a topic of great interest to me in those days and so I went. Besides, he had what I considered to be a truly remarkable business: he was a philanthropical adviser. He made his money telling rich people to whom they should give their money.

I felt certain that once I saw him, the memory of our meeting would come back to me, but that wasn't the case. The man was a stranger, albeit a very pleasant one. He ordered the crab cakes for me, saying they were an absolute imperative unless I was avoiding shellfish for reasons of allergies or religion, which I wasn't. We ate in the more casual restaurant in the club's basement, which was very private, wood paneled, and decorated exclusively with oil paintings of naked women. The paintings were quite good, though I thought the place would have benefited from a seascape or two to break things up.

The philanthropists' adviser was a man in his middle sixties who had a friendly, avuncular air and a Hermès tie. Before the crab cakes reached the table, he made his point. "I think that you should never have to worry about money again," he said.

"There's a thought," I said.

"A talent like yours—" He closed his eyes and shook his head. "You should be protected, taken care of. Your mind shouldn't be cluttered up with paying bills. You should be free to work."

"I'm pretty free now," I said. The Bunting gave me more money than I had ever made and for the first time in my life I didn't make it a point to only go to matinees.

"You'll get the Whiting Award next year," he said. "That is absolutely a given. I know the judging committee. Unless something goes very wrong, I think I can guarantee that."

I took a sip of wine to push back whatever little yipping noise I might have been inclined to make. The Whiting Award was $30,000. This was no small piece of news.

"But there's also a discretionary fund," he said, tenting his fingers. "My discretion. I can write you a check for ten thousand dollars this afternoon. It would disqualify you from winning a Whiting, but ten thousand would mean you wouldn't have to worry about anything for now."

"I'm not worried about anything," I said. "I have money."

"Come back to my office," he said. "I'll write you a check."

I remembered when I was sick as a child and got to stay home from school watching game shows in my mother's bed. The core dilemma of *Let's Make a Deal* was that to have a chance at the big prize, you had to risk the smaller prize you already had. Everything was a risk to be calculated. Of course the other catch was that you had to humiliate yourself in some way to catch the attention of the host, dress like a chipmunk or a toilet bowl.

"I'll wait and see if I win the Whiting," I said.

He smiled at me as if I had passed the first test. "Smart," he said, and I was pleased to think he was proud of me.

The philanthropists' adviser thought I was a genius, an American original. He had never met anyone like me and he told me so. Not only did he want to come up with a plan by which my brilliance would receive a lifetime of funding, he wanted me to be his talent scout. Who did I know who deserved fellowships? What institutions would I like to see doused in cash? Could I come back to the city next week for lunch?

I would like to think that had it just been me, I might have caught on to the game a little bit sooner, but the idea that I could be the philanthropists' adviser's plucky mole made me absolutely giddy. I dropped my bag off at Lucy's and rushed uptown. When I went to the Lotos Club the next week with my address book, the attractive woman at the front desk remembered me and said, "Hello, Miss Patchett." I had plenty of friends who needed money, friends whose brilliant work might never be realized without a little help with the rent. Over a nice salad Niçoise, I turned over their names, addresses, phone numbers, work samples. I told him about Lucy and Adrian and Elizabeth. I arranged for him to meet with the head of the Bunting Institute because they could use some extra funding themselves. The philanthropists' adviser called me on the phone in the evenings after work to go over his notes. He wrote me letters and confided in me about the problems he had with one of his sons. He said he thought of me as a friend and what a lovely surprise that was for him. He was lonely and I understood him. I was honored to be able to understand him.

BACK IN BOSTON, Lucy called me late one night. "Come to the city," she said. "I'm pregnant."

"Ah, hell," I said, sitting down on the bed.

"I really didn't even know I could get pregnant."

"Seems like a bad way to have to find out. Do we need to have that talk about birth control?"

"No, it was just an accident." Lucy had a steady boyfriend then, a sweet guy of the sort who would accompany his girlfriend to an abortion clinic.

"He isn't going with you?"

"I want you to go," she said. "If anything happened, I'd be better off with you."

The next morning I was on my way out the door for an early train when the phone rang. "I need you to come to the city," the philanthropists' adviser said to me with a fair amount of urgency. "I need you to come today."

I told him that in fact I was coming in today.

"Were you not planning on telling me?"

"I wasn't actually, no. I'm coming in to see a friend."

"I just read your galleys," he said. "We have to talk about this book." It was my second novel. He had been very anxious to read it, so anxious that I wondered if a large chunk of my fate was hanging on his opinion of the work. I had gotten him an advance reader's copy from my publisher. I told him I would call him when I got in.

When I arrived, Lucy said she had scheduled her abortion for the next morning. There was a book party for Dennis McFarland at six and she wanted to go. "Meet me there," she said. "He's a great guy and he has the greatest kids."

"I have to meet with my philanthropist."

"Oh," she said dreamily, "your philanthropist. You promise that you told him all about your talented friend?"

"Everything."

"Go have a drink with your philanthropist and then meet me uptown."

"I don't know Dennis McFarland," I said. "I can't crash his book party."

"You won't be crashing, you'll be with me." She wrote the address down on a piece of paper and we promised to meet at six. Then I called the philanthropists' adviser to make our plans.

"Meet me at the polar bear cage in Central Park," he said. "I'll bring a thermos of martinis."

"What?"

"The polar bears."

"No," I said, feeling something dismal bloom in my chest. "I need to be on the Upper East Side. We'll just meet at the Lotos Club." We always met at the Lotos Club.

"No," he said quickly. "They're painting the bar. We'll go to the Polo Club. Have you been to the Polo Club before?"

I had not.

"That's perfect," he said. "I'll have your martini waiting for you."

It was not an unusual story or even an interesting one, but when the punch line came it devastated me nevertheless. No one was in the Polo

Club at four o'clock in the afternoon except for the bartender and the man waiting to meet me. When I walked in, the philanthropists' adviser kissed me on the mouth and I knew the fun was up. He took my hand and told me that he could neither eat nor sleep, that I had destroyed his sense of equilibrium, his happiness. My new novel had revealed to him how completely we were soul mates. Had I ever been to Tanzania? He would take me there. We would go there immediately. We would go in the morning. I scooted down the banquette towards the next table and he dragged along behind me, clutching my arm. Didn't I see what I had done to him? Didn't I know that this was completely my responsibility?

"No," I said.

He drank his martini. He drank mine and ordered two more. The drinks were delivered two tables down from the one we started off at because I kept inching away from him and he kept inching behind me. "Is the problem Tanzania? Do you not want to go to Africa? It will always be there. We can go to Africa later. I'll take you to Vienna, then. You told me you loved Vienna."

I stood up and he pulled me back to the table. "You cannot leave me. I won't let you. I will follow you for the rest of my life."

I was not an American original or a genius or even a writer. I was a moderately pretty woman of thirty who was a good listener and for that it seemed there was a different class of philanthropy. "I'm going to go to the bathroom," I said. "I am going to stay there until you leave."

When I got up he was red-faced and crying and the crying made him look much older. I locked myself in a stall of the women's room at the Polo Club and cried myself for being such a terrible idiot, for being so vain as to have ever thought that things could have been otherwise. I stayed locked in for more than an hour and when I came out he was gone.

I called Lucy from the pay phone to tell her I couldn't meet her, but there was no answer. I was supposed to be at the book party in twenty minutes. If I simply didn't show up, she would worry and so I checked the address in my purse and went even farther uptown, still blurry with anger and shame, thinking I would simply walk in, whisper the facts of my situation to her, and leave discreetly. As I raced up Madison, I remembered every lavish compliment I had received from the philanthropists' adviser and wondered how stupid a person could be to believe such things. I remembered the dress I was wearing the night we met at the Whiting Award and I thought of my friends who would never get funded now. Lucy! For all I knew, she could wind up being blackballed, too. She wouldn't have locked herself in the bathroom of the Polo Club. She would have polished off her own martinis. She would have seen the whole thing as a ridiculous adventure, an opportunity ripe for the taking. She'd be halfway to Tanzania now, having managed to ditch the philanthropists' adviser at Kennedy Airport, while I stood there wringing my parochial hands, feeling cheapened.

I arrived at the party at six o'clock, exactly on time. It was the sort of enormous and elegant brick building I had walked past for years but had never actually been inside of. The doorman sent me up to the twelfth floor in the quiet hum of the wood-paneled elevator. I rang the bell.

Lucy wasn't at the party. It didn't take long to figure that out as there weren't more than a dozen people gathered. I explained the applicable bit of my circumstances: Lucy Grealy had invited me to come with her, we were meeting there, she would arrive in just a minute.

The hostess let me in and introduced me to Dennis McFarland and his family and the few close friends who were there to celebrate the publication of his second novel, which I had not read. They looked at me with polite skepticism and offered me a drink. I accepted with real need. "She'll be here any second," I said. "I called her. She must have already left. The subway this time of night—" But there was no sense in finishing the sentence.

After twenty minutes I asked politely if I might use the phone and called her again, and I tried again twenty minutes after that. Neither Lucy nor her answering machine picked up. My head was reeling with philanthropy. I was wondering if he could ruin me. I was wondering if he had ruined anybody else. I remembered a day we had lunch at the Lotos Club. He was putting an attractive young woman in a taxi just as I was walking up the street. He did not introduce us and she did not look happy. My lifetime ability to make polite conversation had completely abandoned me and I concentrated on killing Lucy the minute I got back to her apartment. After an hour and three glasses of wine there was nothing to do but beg forgiveness and slink towards the door. "I've made some terrible mistake," I told the hostess.

"It's fine," she said with real kindness and patted my arm. It was clear I hadn't pocketed any of the expensive silver knickknacks that were sitting out on the side tables. I was free to go.

It was nearly midnight when Lucy came home. She slammed the door and threw her body back against it. "What a day!" she cried.

"Tell me you were kidnapped," I said from my bed on the sofa. "Nothing else is going to fly with me."

"I wish I'd been kidnapped, it's worse than that."

"You didn't go to the party."

"The party?" She clutched her head. "That was the least of my problems."

It was, I realized, the least of my problems as well, but I was still furious about it. Then Lucy told me she had been on her way out the door to meet me when a friend called to say she was going to commit suicide. What could she have done? She spent the whole evening on the phone and once things had calmed down a little, she had gone to her friend's apartment to try and soothe her. So I couldn't be angry after all. Suicide threats trump everything, book parties and philanthropists' advisers' advances and even pregnancy. We stayed up half the night telling our stories.

"The bastard," Lucy said again and again. "The bastard."

WHEN THE PHONE RANG at seven it came as a real surprise. It felt like we had been asleep for fifteen minutes. Lucy's friends were famous for calling at three and four in the morning, hours I perceived to be unreasonable, but they didn't call at seven. "It's for you," she cried sleepily.

"We're going to Tanzania," the philanthropists' adviser said. "The car is downstairs."

"How did you get this number?"

"Don't worry about packing. Don't worry about anything. Just walk out the door. I've bought your clothes for you. I've arranged for a passport."

"I didn't tell you where I was staying. How do you know where I am?"

"Just come downstairs. I'm in the car. I'm right outside. We're ready to go."

"You're bluffing," I said. "You don't know where I am."

"I will always know where you are," he said gravely. I hung up the phone.

"That's very creepy," Lucy said. She was still holding the extension.

Immediately the phone started to ring like an alarm clock and I told Lucy not to pick it up. In fact my phone would ring for months after that, sometimes every hour on the hour until I finally unplugged it and put it in the closet.

"Pet, look at the time."

"Take your shower first," she said. "I have to go back to sleep."

I crawled off the sofa and took my shower and then shouted up the ladder to Lucy's loft. "Get up! We need to get going."

"I'm too sleepy," she said. "I can't."

"Get up!"

"Forget it," she said. "I'm tired. I can't. I'll have the baby."

"Get up now or get up for the rest of your life."

Lucy moaned and dragged herself out of bed and crawled down the ladder. "That sort of puts it in perspective."

In the days before *Roe v. Wade,* I doubt that many American women were wracked with guilt over having abortions. They were too busy wondering if they were going to be butchered. So when luck went their way and they made it through the procedure safely, it was a cause for celebration rather than remorse. What legalized abortion brought to this country, along with safe medical practices, was the expectation of shame, the need to wonder if you were doing the right thing even though you knew exactly what you'd do in the end. We could have our abortions but we had to feel horrible for the decision we made, even if it was hardly a decision at all. So while social decency compels me to say that on the train uptown we cried and cursed fate and wondered what life might be like with a baby, the truth is we did not. I could not imagine Lucy looking after a baby for an afternoon, much less a life-time. She did not try to imagine it at all. She was a little worried it might hurt. She was wondering when she would be able to have sex again. She was excited because this was also the day she got to go and pick up her book jacket cover.

We went to the fourth floor of a good Park Avenue address and filled out the endless paperwork, then paid in cash. Lucy, so used to being the star in any medical setting, was simply told to take her num-

ber and she would be called. The waiting room was large and nonde-
script. It was full up with guilty-looking teenage boys who wore baseball caps pulled low on their foreheads and kept their eyes fixed on the
television. I found it touching that they had come at all.

When they called Lucy's name, she went to the door and then
turned around and came back to me. I had never even considered the
possibility of second thoughts. "Go to Houghton Mifflin and pick up
the cover," she said. "That way it will be here when I come out."

"Sure," I said.

"But don't look. I don't want you to see it before me."

"I won't look."

She kissed me and then stopped again at the door to wave good-
bye. It was only one more sad medical procedure, one more needle sliding into her blue vein.

It was still impossibly early for all that had happened. I decided to
walk to the publishers' offices on lower Park Avenue. Lucy's editor
gave me the cover in an envelope. I didn't look. I took it back to the
abortionist's, where I was told that Lucy was fine and that she would
be out in a little while. There had been a turnover in the waiting room
as the girls started drifting out, pale and wobbly, while new boys filed
in with new girls who kept their eyes on the floor. Lucy came out looking nearly translucent, a lavender jellyfish, and I took her in my arms.

"It's a factory in there," she said. "They showed us a movie. We
were all lined up on gurneys. And it hurt."

I held up the envelope. "I got the cover."

"Don't open it here," she said, pushing down my hand. "That
would be a bad association."

So we walked out onto Park, where the sky had turned overcast and
gray. We sat on a low wall two buildings away and Lucy opened the
envelope. It was gorgeous. There was her life, *Autobiography of a*

*Face,* with a picture of a little girl on the cover holding a piece of cello-
phane across her face. It could have been Lucy.

We screamed for the sheer joy of what was to come, for the beauty
of what we held in our hands. Lucy, woozy from the medication, kept
one arm around my neck and I kept one arm around her waist and we
stumbled down the street like a pair of morning drunks, glancing up
for taxis, staring at the jacket of her book.

"I wrote a book," she sang. "I wrote a book!"

I didn't win a Whiting Award the next year, but Lucy did.

## Chapter Ten

"COME OVER," LUCY SAID, AS IF I LIVED DOWN THE street. "I'm going to be on the Today show and I don't have anything to wear."

I had never seen what fame looked like up close. I had met a few people who had had it for a while, who had already figured out a comfortable way to wear the suit and make it look smart, but I had never seen it gearing up before or heard the rumble of the machinery that made the wave. I had also never really thought about how abundantly prepared Lucy was to be famous. It was as if the part was written for her. Of course. Now instead of everyone thinking they knew her, they actually would in a sense. She would be recognized not just for her face but for her work. She would land a sea of invitations. There would be possibilities to do interesting things and have heated conversations and drink champagne and be on television and never, never be alone again. It made such perfect sense I couldn't believe that there had been so many years when she hadn't been famous.

*But god damn it, I want to be famous, I'm determined. That's the great thing about writing, as a lifestyle I mean. You can be real down and out but still have some sort of dignity—if you do keep writing that is. Okay, that's it; I'm stopping this letter right now to get some writing done. I love you.*

"What does one wear on television?" Lucy said, pushing through her closet.

I started picking up little balls of clothing off the floor and shaking them out. "Can you at least tell me what's clean and what's dirty so I don't have to start sniffing at things?"

She looked suspiciously at the cardigan I was holding. "Dirty," she said.

I edged inside the closet and began kicking the contents of the floor into the kitchen.

"Don't bring out everything!" Lucy said.

"How else will we have any idea what you have?" I sat down in a pile of crushed fabric and started going through the dresses. Lucy and I, it has already been established, differed in matters of housekeeping and we entered the whole thing with a stand of no judgment, no blame. I wanted to clean out her closet; she wanted me to clean out her closet. Neither of us pretended it was otherwise.

There was a vast collection of unwashed thrift-store dresses with tiny waists and sweetheart necklines, checks and plaids and sentimental flowers, but every one had a stain or a tear or a hanging hem, and while I could sew, I couldn't imagine bringing anything up to the standards of television. Lucy rarely wore the dresses anyway. She bought them for the sheer pleasure she took in knowing that no one else could fit into them. Lucy looked good in jeans, but jeans would not save the day. I told her we were going to Barney's.

"I'm not going to Barney's."

"It's either that or we spend the whole day shopping. This is going to be easier."

And so we got on the subway heading north. The afternoon was bright and hot and Lucy adored hot weather. Half-dried leaves hung limply on every tree in Midtown. At that moment we were perfect, with everything that was good still ahead of us. We locked arms, walked into the store, and went upstairs to approach the racks. It was for me the place where Lucy slipped into her fame. It was the last time I remember her being nervous about anything having to do with success. Before long a woman came up and asked us what we were looking for. She was older, and seemed both sensible and sensibly dressed.

"I need something to wear on television," Lucy said hesitantly.

The woman nodded. "What show?"

She did not doubt us for a second and in giving us the gift of her belief, she made everything true. Lucy in her jeans and T-shirt was a perfectly plausible TV guest. She could have been a rock star.

"*Today*," Lucy said.

The woman looked at Lucy's body, appraising her size, and steered her to a dressing room. "I'll bring you something," she said.

Many outfits and many cups of coffee later, Lucy left the store with a navy blue silk sleeveless tunic top, some very fitted camel-colored pants, and a pair of chunky brown shoes that showed off her elegant ankles. I thought she looked absolutely beautiful, but she never wore any of it again after the show. By then she had figured out television and how to look both good and like herself. But she kept that outfit. Every time I cleaned out her closets over the years I found it there and she would touch it fondly and remember one of the last times in her life that she didn't know any better where the media was concerned.


WHEN SHE WAS in the mood, and usually she was, Lucy could be both natural and forthcoming. She had a great ability to be herself, if she was giving an interview or walking down Canal Street, and because of that people flocked to her. The models and supermodels called out to her as they teetered home over SoHo's cobblestone streets in the small hours of the morning, "Hey, Lucy! Good night!" It was just like Iowa and it was nothing like Iowa at all. Lucy started doing publicity months before the publication of *Autobiography of a Face,* and she kept it up for more than a year after the book came out in hardback and another year for the paperback after that. She loved all of it. She loved the airports and the hotels. She loved being able to say that the Alexis was her favorite hotel in Seattle and the best tiramisu was at the Four Seasons in Atlanta. She loved the bookstores and the people who stood in line holding her book to their chests, to say how much they loved her. She especially loved being interviewed and having the host confide in her when it was over that she was the favorite, the best. She loved having her hair brushed and her forehead powdered for the lights. She loved producers and stylists and cameras, even though she complained about them all. She loved throwing her suitcase inside the door and saying, "My God, the traffic!" or "This schedule is going to kill me!" or "That flight!" and then she would drop onto the couch, roll her eyes and smile and say, "I love it."

Lucy was in fashion magazines; she was the subject of an entire article in *People.* One particularly memorable shoot was done in the country and she had her picture taken draped over the back of a white horse. Then, in full makeup, she shucked off all her clothes and scampered up the limbs of a high tree. She draped herself across a branch, arms and legs dangling, eyes closed, while on the ground the photographer snapped away. For years she had one of those pictures on her refrigerator and it was stunningly beautiful, black and white, somehow Victorian if naked Victorian women ever shinnied up trees. She was playing the part of a sleeping wood nymph in the bend of a wooden arm. But then she brought some guy home one night and while she wasn't looking, he slid the photograph from its magnet and took it away.

*        *        *

LUCY WAS PARTIAL to Charlie Rose for a television interview and she liked Lenny Lopate on the radio. She was doing such a good job talking about her book that she was also called on to talk about other things. One day she could be discussing the survival of tragedy with Oprah and the next it was America's obsession with beauty on CNN. The CNN interview played live and when she left the studio and got on the subway to go home, a girl tapped on her arm. Lucy looked up from her newspaper. "Weren't you on my television ten minutes ago?" the girl said to her. Lucy shrugged. "Probably," she said.

Lucy didn't watch herself on television or listen to her interviews. She could be completely at ease when the tape was rolling but when she saw herself played back, she tore the performance apart. It only had to happen once or twice and then she learned the lesson. When people told her she was great, all she could say was, "Really?"

When I listened to her being interviewed by Terry Gross on the NPR program *Fresh Air,* it seemed perfectly clear why she wouldn't want to hear it.

"Many of us are dissatisfied when we look in the mirror," Terry Gross's introduction of Lucy began, "but that's different from the extreme anguish Lucy Grealy experienced when she saw her reflection. By most standards her face was ugly, even repulsive."

Surely the introduction had been taped after the interview and edited in. Surely Lucy had not been sitting in a radio station having to hear the word repulsive applied to her face. I wanted to find her at that exact minute, wrap her up in my arms. Never repulsive, not on her very worst days, not with the tissue expander fully inflated. But maybe Lucy hadn't heard it. She was so completely easy, funny, unflappable while she talked. She opened up by reading a section from her book. And there it was—her word, not Terry Gross's. "If feeling like a freak had been more in my mind than in my face at other times in my life, the visage I saw staring back at me was undeniably repulsive."

"A lot of my suffering was emotional suffering," she said on the radio. "I mean, there was a definite physical side to it, there was a large physical side to it, but I saw that as rather easy compared to the sort of emotional assault of guilt and shame that I was continuously throwing upon myself.

"[My face] changed weekly practically, which was part of the, you know, the story, the dilemma. My story is really not so much the story about being disfigured, it's about having a face that changed so continuously that I never really identified myself as connected to it. And the easiest moments in my life, or rather the most damaging moments, have been that easy fall into saying: I'm ugly. Just like defining it and closing the door on it that way, rather than looking at the fact that my face was different, almost continuously, and that I put off developing that sort of social sense that most people have to come to terms with. On the other hand I was always able to feel special. I never had that familiar adolescent worry of fading into the crowd. I was special, and I tried to use that to my advantage, and I tried to use it as a power almost over other people."

Everyone had always recognized Lucy, but now there were people who had seen her, heard her, read her. There were people who were attracted to the unmistakable light put out by a sudden celebrity. On a crowded and glorious autumn afternoon, we walked through SoHo laughing, arms around each other's waists. We had just bought matching leopard-print miniskirts from a sidewalk vendor when a handsome Jamaican man with long braids started riding circles around us on his bicycle. "Beautiful day for beautiful girls," he said.

"You think this day's for us?" Lucy said to him.

"I think this day is for you," he said. He dropped the toe of his tennis shoe lightly to the pavement and kept turning around us. "You two girlfriends?"

"We're girlfriends," Lucy said. "We're not *girlfriends*."

"So you still like boys fine."

"Some of them," Lucy said, starting to lose interest.

"Those sure are pretty shoes. I saw those shoes when you walked by and I thought to myself, I've got to meet the woman who is wearing those shoes."

Her shoes had long leather cords on them that wrapped around her ankles and were tied in a bow. "So now you met her."

"What's her name?"

"I'm Lucy," she said. "You'll find me later."

It was New York, but everyone found her again later on.


LUCY'S FAVORITE rhetorical question was, "Will I ever have sex again?" It was a habit she started in Iowa whenever she was sure she had broken it off with B—— for good. It was the first thing she said to practically anyone who walked in the door. "Will I ever have sex again?" In those days she especially enjoyed calling up our friend Jono from college and asking him because she thought as a man he had a better shot of knowing for sure. But it stuck. She had simply gotten into the habit of asking, and whenever she had gone more than three days without having sex, she started polling her friends again. I was so in the habit of answering her that when another friend of mine broke up with her boyfriend and said to me, "May I ask you a question?" I answered her without even thinking, "Of course you'll have sex again." She was horrified.

Lucy had plenty of other questions as well: "Do you love me?"

"You think I'm pretty, don't you?" "Do you think I'm a good writer?"
But the odd part was they were all so interchangeable. What all of the
questions really meant was, "Everything is going to be okay, right?"
Still, the sex question was her favorite. Sometimes months would go by
in which she would ask me every day.

"You had sex today," I said. "You aren't allowed to ask me on a
day when you've already had sex."

"But I want to know if I'm going to have it *again.*"

Sometimes Lucy seemed shameless, which is to say she wasn't bur-
dened by the same notions of what is shameful and what is moral and
what is right that I was. Or maybe it's that we all have a certain allot-
ment of shame within us and Lucy spent hers on other things. She was
ashamed of the way she ate. She felt enormous shame at the idea of
having food on her chin or breaking out into a sweat when she swallowed. She was ashamed of her teeth because she could not close her
mouth. She was ashamed of her eyelid, which had stayed swollen off
and on ever since that surgery in Aberdeen. It drove her crazy and she
was certain that everyone noticed it. I told her constantly that those
were things she should in no way be ashamed of, that shame should be
reserved for the things we choose to do, not the circumstances that life
puts on us. But it was all just a matter of opinion. Telling yourself you
shouldn't be ashamed of something rarely got anyone anywhere.
Because Lucy was at times ashamed of the way that she looked, she
seemed to have no shame left over for sex. For sex she was fearless, and
the world seemed able to smell it on her. She could be standing in line
in a coffee shop in the middle of winter, wearing jeans and a heavy
jacket, a cap pulled low on her head, and sure enough some guy would
start to tell her how he had such a strong feeling she was an interesting
person and the next thing they knew they were out of the coffee line. If
she shared a cab with a man on a corner, they often wound up at the

same destination. One night, at the height of her fame, she was putting the key in the front door of her apartment when an eighteen-year-old boy in a doorman uniform tapped her on the shoulder. He told her in mediocre English that she had walked by the building where he worked on the Upper East Side that very night and he had felt an overwhelming sense of love for her. He had left his post and followed her down into the subway, on the train to SoHo, and walked behind her to her door, all the while trying to get up the courage to talk to her. Now here he was, declaring his feelings for her. She thought about it for a minute and then invited him up.

Heriberto came around off and on for the next year. He was a sweet kid, and better than that, he was a great story.

"I hate to say it, but I probably would have called the police," I said.

"Then you would have missed out," Lucy said.


SEVERAL MONTHS AFTER the publication of Lucy's book, when she was the toast of both popular culture and all things literary, my second novel, *Taft*, came out. In the same way all the rumblings that preceded *Autobiography of a Face* made it clear that it was going to be a big book, the comparative silence surrounding this novel made it clear that it was going to sink without a trace. It had an awful title (my fault) and an awful cover (my publishers' fault), and despite getting the best reviews I'd had, it did not seem to be selling outside of my immediate family. When I was scheduled to give a reading in New York, Lucy suggested that we team up, appear as a double bill, and then afterwards she would throw us a big book party at her loft. We had the same publisher and the same publicist and so they were more than happy to oblige us as everyone stood to benefit. She was my best friend, and she was lending me the brilliance of her light in a moment when things were looking decidedly dull for me. It was something we did for one another over the years, depending on which of us had more light to share. At the beautiful and now departed downtown Rizzoli's, the dozen or so Ann Patchett fans squeezed in among the Lucy Grealy throng of well over two hundred. Not that anyone was keeping score. They had printed up bookmarks with both of our pictures on them. There we were, tucked together inside every book sold at Rizzoli's that night. The manager hid us upstairs, away from the crowd, so that we could make a sweeping entrance. We crouched together between some bookshelves and listened to the buzz of voices, laughing to think they were all waiting on us. Lucy was famous, and I was famous for being with her.

There was a lot of cancer in the room that night, cancer in the process of being defeated and cancer in the process of defeating people. There were the ravages that cancer, long gone, had left in its wake, including the damage it had done to Lucy. I was able to assess in a matter of seconds that the crowd had not come to hear fiction, any fiction. I was the warm-up act. I read for five minutes, answered two questions, and got back in my seat so that I could see the show we had all come for. Lucy got up and read, her little voice as always reminding me of the girl who had announced the films at Sarah Lawrence. She was a natural in front of an audience.

There was no underestimating the power of *Autobiography of a Face*. From the moment I had read the essay that would later become the book, I knew that this was the place that Lucy's enormous heart and great intelligence would dovetail into the piece of art she had always hoped to make. I read the book as a pile of pages, and again for copyediting, again in galleys and again when it was published and every time it had shown me a greater depth. Every time it found a way to move me all over again, not because she was my friend but because it was such a beautiful book.

After the crowd was able to control their weeping after hearing the passage she read about being tortured by schoolboys in stairwells, she opened the floor for questions.

"You were so incredibly brave," a woman began. "If it were me, I wouldn't have been able to survive it."

"Meaning what, you would have died?" Lucy said. "It doesn't work that way, unless you kill yourself."

People said it to Lucy all the time. They said it to me about Lucy. It was meant as some sort of compliment and yet it never quite came off that way. It sounded as if by merely living, she had become a conspirator with her fate. My brave and heroic Lucy made it clear to the audience that she had no interest in being anybody's inspiration. She was not there as a role model for overcoming obstacles. She was a serious writer, and she wanted her book to be judged for its literary merit and not its heartbreaking content. When people raised their hands to ask a question, more often than not the question turned out to be a statement of what they themselves had endured. Lucy refused to let the evening digress into a litany of battle stories.

"Most of the time I forget I even had cancer," she said. "That's not the part of the story I'm interested in."

"When I got my own diagnosis," a woman started, and Lucy listened with moderate patience. When the speaker was finished, Lucy only nodded and pointed to the next hand that was raised.

"It's amazing how you remember everything so clearly," a woman said, her head wrapped up in a bright scarf. "All those conversations, details. Were you ever worried that you might get something wrong?"

"I didn't remember it," Lucy said pointedly. "I wrote it. I'm a writer."

This shocked the audience more than her dismissal of illness, but she made her point: she was making art, not documenting an event. That she chose to tell her own extraordinary story was of secondary importance. Her cancer and subsequent suffering had not made this book. She had made it. Her intellect and ability were in every sense larger than the disease.

At the end we went and sat together at a table where Lucy signed a seemingly endless number of books and I signed a handful. Her fans were a sensitive bunch and many of them bought a copy of my book because I was just sitting there and Lucy was so busy. They slipped her letters and cards; someone brought her flowers. Lucy nodded politely, but her fan mail was too depressing to bear. More often than not it was a one-upmanship of illness, a report from the suffering sweepstakes that would show Lucy how she had not been the winner after all. I tried to read the bag of letters beside her desk once, but by the third one I felt nearly suicidal, as if the world was a blister of grief with only the thinnest layer of tightly stretched skin holding everything in place. The smallest touch, the lightest reminder, and everything was brought to the surface again.

What a shame these people weren't around in Scotland or during her childhood, through the endless boring hours spent in hospital beds or throwing up after chemotherapy. Now everyone was turning out to take communion in Lucy's sadness when in fact all we wanted was to get through the line because there was a party to go to, our party, and we had cases of wine and champagne stacked up in the bathtub back on Mercer Street. The sadness, it seemed, was finally over at the exact moment that everyone wanted to share it.

Lucy had hired a student to stand on the street outside her building and open the downstairs door and direct people up the stairs. Stuart had opened up his enormous loft next to hers for dancing while Lucy's side was for food and conversation, although how much conversation could there be with the music so loud? It seemed that everyone we had ever known from college and Iowa and Provincetown and the Bunting had all moved to New York and they all knew each other in some vague way and were thrilled to be reunited. It was a wonderful party. Our publisher had sent over boxes of our books and they constituted all of our decorations. We gave them out with every glass of wine and signed them with extravagant pledges of love. When we got tired of signing our own books, we signed each other's. I introduced two of my old boyfriends to one another and they became such good friends that when one of them married years later, the other was his best man. Lucy was yelling at people, trying to make them dance. It was impossible to even think of a party at Lucy's that did not involve dancing. When she couldn't get anyone to join her, she turned the Talking Heads up loud and started in by herself. She took to the floor like a firefly, moving so easily I would have thought she was in our kitchen back in Iowa, and still no one would dance, but now she was having fun and she couldn't have cared less.

## Chapter Eleven

IN THE FEW MOMENTS OF MY BUNTING FELLOWSHIP
when I wasn't in New York or in the pool at Harvard, I was doing
research for a nonfiction book I planned to write about the Los Angeles Police Department. Since I had to be out of my apartment in Cambridge at the end of August, I decided I would use Nashville as home
base until I finished up the book tour for *Taft* and then I would head
west. But once I got back to Tennessee, I met a man named Karl Van-
Devender, whom my mother worked for. After a few dates, I decided
we were having such a nice time that it wouldn't hurt to delay my
plans. It would be all the same if I left in a few weeks. Then it was a few
months. I took an apartment with a six-month lease, and then I
renewed the lease.

I certainly did not set out to find a man of whom my best friend
would approve, but Karl was Lucy's dream come true. He was older, he
was kind, he was handsome, he was intelligent, he was generous, and
most importantly, he was a doctor. Lucy's relationship to doctors was
as complicated and nuanced as her medical history. They were the ultimate father figures of her youth and for a few kind words about how
brave she was, she would gladly neglect to mention her pain. They
were the busy, important men (and all of the pivotal doctors in Lucy's
life, to the best of my knowledge, were men) who occasionally sat on

her bed and stroked her forehead, handsome men who for the briefest moment paid all of their valuable attention to her. They told her she was the most remarkable case they had seen and made promises of how they would shepherd her through to a better life. The surgeons stoked her deepest dreams of repair like coal men shoveling fuel into a roaring furnace. They told her not to worry about the money, and then presented her with enormous bills. They told her it would take three surgeries over six months, only to discover it was ten surgeries over three years. There were wonderful doctors, full of compassion and innovation, but they never seemed able to consider any surgery but the one they were about to perform. They never took her lifetime into account or figured in the enormous costs, physically, financially, and emotionally, of all that had failed so dismally before. They didn't account for Lucy, only for her face. And maybe they couldn't. She was too huge for casual consideration. But how can you operate on the face without understanding what the face means to the girl? How can the meaning of kissing, swallowing, speaking, be completely ignored in favor of mechanics? The doctors took what they needed from her body, sometimes without ever mentioning it, so even though her head was swollen beyond recognition, what she cried over was the scar running up her leg where some surgeon had taken a vein without asking. She loved her pretty legs.

But these were the doctors I felt kindly towards, the ones who, even if they couldn't see the bigger picture, genuinely wanted to help her. There were another kind as well, the ones for whom Lucy was a superstar challenge, the ones who had a new vascular technique to try out, the ones with no follow-through but a large prescription of OxyContin. Those were the ones she called cowboys because there was always a trace of a swagger in their fast walk. They didn't answer questions or return calls, and whatever flash of attention they gave was born of noblesse oblige. Their dance cards were booked a year in advance and whatever you got you were lucky to have. The hospital hallways were full of them.

But Lucy was a victim neither of neglect nor good intentions. She was absolutely complicit with her doctors. She always meant for surgeons to see her as both a viable candidate and an amazing case, and she was extremely careful never to reveal the depths of her hope or despair to them. Lucy, who lacked obedience in nearly all matters, was as mute as a first-year novice when a doctor spoke. She went to the hospital when she was told. If she had fears or hesitations, she confided in her friends, not her doctors. More than anything she wanted to be the special patient, the favorite, the best. Not only was her case the most compelling, she was the most agreeable. While doctors were often still the dream fathers, now they were the dream dates as well, busy, powerful men peering into her pale blue eyes with pen lights. She fell in love with them and longed for them to fall in love with her. Once Lucy gave a lecture to a convention of plastic surgeons and one came up to her later and suggested she come by his office for a consultation. He had some new ideas that he thought could help her. They made love on the examining table.

"It was my ultimate fantasy," she said. "Except for the part about him being married and an asshole."

Those two points aside, she went back several times. I thought it was nothing short of a miracle that he didn't bill her.

There was still the penultimate fantasy, the one about the father instead of the lover. In this fantasy the doctor tells all his other patients to go home. He has as much time as she could possibly need to say everything she ever wanted to say, to ask every question no matter how trivial or embarrassing it might seem. Then he would invite her home for dinner. His wife and children love her so much they give her the daughter's bedroom. That was the doctor Lucy found in Karl.

I brought Karl to New York to meet Lucy in October of 1994. We agreed to have brunch at a restaurant called the Cupping Room a few blocks away from Lucy's apartment. It was cold and wet and the place was packed full of fat coats taking up extra chairs and the hooks on the walls. Lucy was late, and as I sat there with Karl, I thought maybe I had made a mistake. If she didn't like him, she would tell me and I didn't think I wanted to know. Karl assured me he had met plenty of people in his life and most of them liked him fine.

Ten minutes later Lucy came in pink with fever. Her hair and skin were slightly damp and she was packed into several sweaters. I made the introductions. "I'm sick," she announced as she sat down at the table next to Karl, and she was. She should have been home in bed but she had come out for me, not wanting to miss the chance to meet my new boyfriend.

Karl ordered her tea and rested two fingers on the inside of her wrist. After a minute he touched her forehead.

"I get pneumonia," she said. "Everything goes into my lungs."

And so Karl scooted his chair out and, in that crowded restaurant and before there was any conversation, laid his ear against her back and told her to breathe in. When she did, she looked at me, at first as if to say, What the hell? but when she exhaled she smiled. It was charming, after all, to have a handsome man press his head to your back so soon upon meeting.

"Your lungs are fine," he said.

"Pancakes," she said to the waitress, "undercooked." Then she blew her nose. Karl held out his hand for the Kleenex.

"You want to look in my Kleenex?" she said.

I thought it was going a little too far, but in that moment Lucy blossomed. No one had ever asked to see the contents of her tissue, she told me later, in a hospital or out, though at several points in her life she had hoped that someone would be interested.

Karl wanted to hear Lucy's entire medical history, which was a little bit like asking to hear the political history of China over eggs and toast. He stopped her frequently to ask more questions, to encourage her to make the story longer. We had all day. We could stay through dinner, until they turned the chairs over on the tables and pushed us out with a broom. When the conversation came up to the present, Lucy said that she thought the surgeries were essentially over. They should be over. Except she still needed teeth.

Teeth were always going to be the final chapter of Lucy's surgical history, but no matter how many operations she had they always seemed to hang just outside her reach. She had lost all of her lower teeth and most of her upper teeth save the front ones in the endless rounds of childhood radiation. Life since the age of ten had been spent mashing soft food against the roof of her mouth with her tongue and swallowing what she could with sips of water. She was prone to choking and once had her life saved with a dramatic Heimlich maneuver performed by the poet Tom Lux in a New York steak house. She could have gotten teeth in Scotland, she said, had she been willing to stay there for God only knew how much longer, but that would have constituted another brand of defeat. In the States, teeth were considered a dental matter, even if they had all fallen out due to cancer of the jaw. Dental implants were only covered by dental insurance, something Lucy, like most writers, had never dreamed of having. A single implanted tooth could cost up to $1,500, and there was no way she was ever going to come up with that kind of money.

"We'll get you teeth," Karl said.

"You can't just get a person teeth," Lucy said.

Karl thought she was wrong and he shook his head slightly, as if it were simply a matter of picking up the check for lunch. "I bring people a lot of business, the hospital, other doctors," he said. "People would be glad to do me a favor if I asked. And if worse came to worst, I'd just pay for it myself."

Lucy was exasperated by Karl's reasoning, nearly angry. "You can't make something sound so easy when I haven't been able to do it my whole life," she said. "It isn't easy. It's impossible."

"If it's only a matter of money and finding someone to do it, then it's easy."

After hours and hours of talking, the three of us walked to a pharmacy in the rain and Karl got Lucy some antibiotics to combat the fever and what he considered to be the suspicious contents of her Kleenex. Then we took her back to her apartment and tucked her in for a nap. After we left, I wondered how well I knew Karl. Like Lucy, I found the promise to be uncomfortably extravagant.

A month later Karl sent her a plane ticket to come to Nashville. He had lined up some people to talk to her about teeth.


My mother had an extremely ratty old black cat named Slick that none of us much cared for. I put the cat in the past tense, even though he is at this moment still alive. He is eighteen, half blind, and down to three teeth. The very fact that he shows up for his can of food in the mornings continues to surprise us. The cat loved Lucy, who loved the cat. She would carry him from room to room in my mother's house and beat her open palms rhythmically against his sides. It looked and sounded very much like abuse the way she pounded on him as if he were a dusty couch pillow pinned to a clothesline, but the cat adored his beatings. He purred in rapture, butting her hand with his head whenever she had gotten tired of the game.

*I am taking care of a cat for the cat's protection league, a different one than the last I wrote about. This one was a mess when he came. I've never seen anything so terrified, so lost. He wouldn't eat, wouldn't play, would only cram himself into the darkest hole he could find. I've spent a lot of time with him, though, and he's really changed. He purrs and plays and is curious: I feel like a proud cat psychiatrist. It's good to be reminded that you can do small positive things which make a difference in the world, however small they are. He still won't let you pick him up easily, he seems convinced that every time I go near him I want to make cat stew, but once I get him he is really sweet, curling up around my neck like a scarf and purring in sheer gratitude that I didn't hurt him.*

Lucy knew which cat wanted to be held and which one wanted to be smacked. The weight she put on things so often struck me as backwards, but in some ways she had a deep understanding of the logic of the world. I would have thought that the prospect of getting teeth after twenty years spent without them would have been thrilling or daunting, but she shrugged it off. She had no interest in obsessing over possible outcomes. She would simply go and see what they had to say and that was all there was to do. And she was right.

The oral surgeon sat us down in his office and gave us a glossy book of dental implant surgery. The process was explained to us while we followed along with the pictures. Basically, a metal stake would be implanted into the jaw, one for every tooth. It was a shining hook that jutted up from an angry red gum, the prototype for some as-yet-to-be-written horror film in which the fearsome murderer chews his victims to ribbons. After that, a second surgery attached the tooth to the claw, so forth and so on, a couple of teeth at a time.

"Good God," Lucy said.

"Isn't there another way to go about this?" I asked.

"A denture maybe," she said.

The doctor put Lucy back in the chair and filled her mouth with a bright light. He told me to come around the other side and look. She couldn't open wide at all, but what I could see was a rocky cave, the place where the loose ends of every surgery carelessly came together.

"You can see here there isn't any sort of a plate you could attach a denture to. There's nothing really for it to sit on. It would have to be implants, and even those are going to be tricky."

After he left, Lucy sat up in the pale blue vinyl chair. She unfastened her paper bib from its clip and held it in her hands. She looked shaky and then, in the smallest way, she started to cry.

"I feel so ashamed," she said.

"Ashamed?" I sat down next to her on the sloping seat of the dental chair. "What could you be ashamed of?"

"I've never let a friend look inside my mouth before."

Was that possible? Had I never seen the inside of Lucy's mouth? Was there really still something I hadn't seen?

The oral surgeon sent us to the plastic surgeon, which is where we should have started had we wanted to save everyone some time. She took an X ray of Lucy's jaw and slid it up on the light board. There were twisted pieces of wire holding bone together and spikes in a few of her teeth I didn't know were implants. There was the delicate ghost of the necklace she was wearing. The surgeon, who was pretty and friendly and blond, took a plastic pen out of the pocket of her lab coat and pointed to the mess of her lower jaw. "You don't want implants," she said. "They'd break what's left of the bone getting them in, or if they did get them in, you'd break your jaw chewing. This jaw isn't meant for chewing."

"So what's the alternative?" Lucy said.

The doctor clicked off the light switch and handed her the image of herself. "My best advice is to keep going exactly the way you've been going for as long as you can, unless you want to do another bone graft to build up the lower jaw enough to sink the implants."

It was the kind of news that was easier to take in Tennessee than it would have been in New York. She could pass these doctors off as a couple of rubes who didn't know all the magic the big guns were working back in the city. The trick was finding the right doctor, someone who was fearless and innovative, someone who was willing to risk everything Lucy had, the same way she was willing to risk herself. She tossed the X ray into the backseat of my car.

"Do you mind if I keep that?" I asked her.

She told me she'd be flattered and when we got back to my apartment, we put it up on the refrigerator. There was something about that X ray that looked more like Lucy to me than any picture I had seen.

"I'll call Karl," I told her. "He'll know what to do next."

"There's nothing to do next," she said. She didn't seem especially disappointed. She had been right after all. Karl had underestimated just how complicated she was.

"There's going to be something else to do," I said. I called Karl at his office and told him what had happened.

"Oh, well," he said. "We tried."

But hadn't he been sure? Hadn't he looked her in the eye and said he could make this happen? "Isn't there someone else we can talk to?"

"They're good doctors. If they say it can't be done then it probably can't be done."

It turns out that in the Cupping Room, Karl had spoken to Lucy as a doctor. Lucy and Karl both understood this, but I had thought he was speaking to her as a magician, someone who could make the impossible true.

*          *          *

THAT NIGHT THERE was an engagement party at my mother and her husband's house for my stepsister, Marcie, and Robb, her fiancé. Somehow all the guests had shown up forty-five minutes early, so that when Lucy and I came home (we had stopped off at the movies to shake the doctors out of our heads) we were late. We ran through the party and up the stairs to change clothes while the guests made wedding talk and drank wine. I hated being late, and I changed clothes quickly so I could get back to the kitchen and help my mother pass around the trays of canapés. Once I was dressed, Lucy gave me a hard look of appraisal.

"What?"

"The skirt," she said gravely.

"Too short?" It was short, but I had thought that because it was black and I was wearing it with black tights, it didn't make too much of a statement.

Lucy put her hand on my shoulder. "I only say this because I love you, because you are my best friend in the world."

"Tell me."

"Because if one did not truly love another and feel confident that the love was returned, one could never be completely honest."

"The skirt," I started.

"That's family down there," she said in an instructional whisper, "and you look like a total slut."

The skirt, which wrapped over itself in the front and snapped at the waist, came off easily—no doubt part of its slutty charm. I was out of it in two seconds and stepping into one that was gray and wool and discreetly covered my calves. My mother had married again a couple of years before and my relationship with the new stepfamily downstairs was still uncomfortably polite. It was perfectly reasonable to think that they would see such an insubstantial skirt not as fashionable or stylish but simply, awkwardly cheap. I kissed Lucy's forehead in gratitude. "I love you," I said. "Once again I owe you my life."

Lucy closed her eyes and nodded. "It's all right."

Lucy took a shower while I hurried downstairs into the swirl of family below. Or maybe that wasn't it at all. Maybe my family was upstairs, taking a shower, and I was walking into a party of lovely strangers. Lucy and I were one another's history. I would see her through her quest for teeth and she would tell me when I was about to embarrass myself. What constituted family if not that?

Ten minutes later Lucy came scampering down the stairs looking extremely sexy in high heels, a turtleneck sweater, and my black dinner napkin of a skirt.

"Gotcha," she said.

## Chapter Twelve

LUCY WAS AWFUL WITH MONEY IN A WAY THAT ONE imagines the Marx Brothers or Laurel and Hardy might have been awful with money. There could have been a movie, *Laurel and Hardy Go to the Bank,* in which our heroes try to bring their life savings in for safekeeping but at every turn find themselves distracted: pretty girls, butterflies, squalling children. All the while the money flutters out of their pockets like a careless trail of bread crumbs. In the sequel, *Back to the Bank,* they would mistakenly spit their chewing gum into the big check they were supposed to deposit and then for the rest of the movie they would struggle to undo the sticky damage they had done. That was the way it was with Lucy. She had an almost magnetic pull towards poverty. When she had money, she gave it away or spent it extravagantly. She bought a horse. She took a last-minute trip to Morocco. Money, like everything else, needed to be charmed. It should be surprising in its arrival and stylish in its departure. It should not be budgeted or saved, as those were the notions of working stiffs. Money for Lucy arrived in the form of a check for foreign rights, something that showed up like an unexpected guest, just minutes after she had seen the perfect pair of leather jeans hanging in the window of a SoHo shop. I once found $50,000 in checks stuck to her refrigerator with a magnet.

"I never get to the bank," she said.

"But why on the refrigerator?"

"I just found that check from the Whiting. I thought it would be safe there where I could see it." The $30,000 prize from the Whiting Foundation came in two installments. The check for the first half had gone missing for more than a month and she was dreading having to ask them for a replacement.

A few months before, at the height of her fame, she had run out of cash between royalty checks and had taken a job as a receptionist at a gallery where people were forever coming in and saying, "Didn't I just read your book?"

It was as if there was an open window in her apartment through which piles of crumpled bills blew in and out like leaves. Sometimes when the tides were running in her favor, she would sock money away in a self-employed pension account that exacted huge penalties for early withdrawal, only to pull the money out six months later and pay the fees. Lucy wanted to have the life of a fictional character, and her constant whiplash between champagne and tap water made her seem straight out of a Fitzgerald novel. Caller identification was invented with Lucy specifically in mind, as it was so effective in helping her dodge collection agencies. There was nothing about collection she liked, though she saw it as part of the role of the artist, like the landlord banging on the door in *La Bohème*.

Truly, she wished she had no bills, and there were times the weight of that particular burden pushed her down mightily, but on the other hand, she was very equipped to deal with it. Debt was part of the landscape, a tree or a shrub that added texture to the vista. She had lived beneath the weight of mounting hospitals bills for most of her life. Her student loans were equally monstrous, and while she might have tossed a couple hundred dollars in their direction from time to time to throw them off the scent, she never embraced the coupon booklets of regular payments. So when she finally had some real success, some real money, she decided she was entitled to all of it. She had done without for long enough. She had worked hard and she deserved what was hers. That meant she neglected to pay large portions of her taxes, a debt that increased with every tick of the clock. From time to time Lucy hired tax lawyers to help her sift through the wreckage, but all that did was create a new genre of bills she did not pay: the lawyer bills.

I gave Lucy money, but so did most of her friends. She rotated her needs among us and never asked anyone for too much. "Just a loan until Thursday," she would say. "*Vogue* owes me for an article and I'll have my check by then."

"Don't ask me for a loan," I said, and gave her the money. "I don't ever want to be one more call you avoid picking up."

She didn't give money back, but she gave money to people who had less than she did.

Of course Lucy had a tremendous ability to earn money; it's just that she froze every time she came anywhere near it. Magazine editors called her constantly. Not only was she a great writer with a big name, she'd won a National Magazine Award, which gave her yet another layer of clout with which to drive up her fees. But she was better about accepting assignments than she was about finishing them. She could get tied into a knot over a two-thousand-word article for *Allure,* avoiding the editor's phone calls as assiduously as the bill collectors'. She loved exotic assignments. She once took a job for a women's sports magazine in which she rode a horse alone across Ireland through rain and muck and bogs with only a simple map and verbal directions to get her from one farmhouse to the next. But writing the article proved to be torture that took months of editorial harassment.

"How many people could ride a horse alone across Ireland?" I said in one of my standard pep talks. "You've already done the impossible part. Just write it up."

But magazine work was just the little fish. What she really needed to write, what everyone wanted her to write for the big money, was a proposal for a new book. She didn't have to write the book itself, at least not for a while. All she needed to come up with was a little piece of it, twenty pages. Even less than twenty pages. The world had finally caught on to what I had known since I was seventeen: Lucy Grealy was one of the more compelling people around. People wanted to hear whatever she had to say.

"I'm going to write a book about tango," she said. "I've signed up for lessons from the same school Robert Duvall studied at."

"That sounds good."

"The history of tango, learning the tango, tango as metaphor. It's all very sexual."

So Lucy danced. She liked the part when the instructor dominated her, slung her head back until it nearly grazed the floor, but on the next song *she* wanted to be the one who got to do the slinging. It didn't work that way. Every time she strapped on her shoes, the book became a little less interesting to her, and after a while she dropped the idea altogether. One night, about a year later, we gave a reading together in Provincetown where we were both teaching in the summer program at the Fine Arts Work Center. We were living together in a big apartment on the bottom floor of a converted barn that was always full of the sand that we tracked in from our afternoons at the beach. "What are you going to read?" I asked.

"The tango essay."

"I didn't know you ended up writing about tango."

"It isn't really much about the tango," she said. "It's inspired by the tango." She hopped up and stomped out a few impressive dance steps, then she arched her back and raised her hands above her head.

I read first. If my life had had any learning curve, I knew enough to never try to follow Lucy in anything. I always loved coming back to Provincetown, and I loved reading at the Work Center in a way that I don't enjoy reading nearly so much anyplace else. It was the place where everything in my life had turned around. It was where Lucy and I had both written our first books. To be there together on a clear hot night in July reading from my third book was complete joy. It was the book I had dedicated to Lucy and Elizabeth McCracken.

When I was finished, Lucy leaned over and gave me a kiss. When she went up to the podium, I thought how funny it was that I was going to hear what she had written for the first time, just like every other member of the audience. She was wearing a little blue knit top with a white stripe down the center that we had bought that afternoon and she looked like summer, tan and blond. "Hey," she said to the audience, as if she had just walked into the room and was pleased and surprised to find us there.

"Hey!" we said to Lucy.

She read the tango essay, which was, as she had told me, only nominally about tango. It was more about sex, the seemingly conflicting desires to dominate and be dominated. It was about the relationship between Morticia and Gomez Addams, the characters on *The Addams Family* whose passions were forever sweeping them away into tango. It was about picking up a guy in a bar in the East Village and how they took a *Cosmo* sex quiz together and how she confirmed that yes, it was true, women could have unlimited orgasms. When he said he didn't believe her, she took him back to her apartment, sat him at the foot of her bed, and showed him it was possible—seventeen times.

As I listened I felt, in no particular order, that I couldn't believe that Lucy had masturbated all night in front of a stranger; I couldn't believe she'd never told me that it had happened; I couldn't believe she'd written about it and then read it to a roomful of strangers on a night that we were reading together. Shock is not a particularly sustaining response to literature, but I was shocked by all of it. Like the act itself, the story went from something that was briefly sexy, to something that was grinding and mechanical, to something that was embarrassing and, finally, exhausting. Because we were in Provincetown, where only the night before one of my students had read a story about shaving his testicles while talking on the phone to his mother, I was the only one who so much as blinked.

"You could have told me what you were reading," I said to her on our way to dinner. I was angry at her, but my anger only made me feel like a prude.

"Bubala," she said, leaning her head against my shoulder, "you're mad at me."

"Not mad," I lied.

"I've offended your sensibilities," she said. "Forgive me." I could tell in the darkness from the lilt of her voice that she was pleased.

When Lucy published her tango essay under the title "What It Takes" in her collection *As Seen on TV,* the masturbation scene was considerably shorter and this time took place not with a stranger from a bar but with a friend with whom she had wagered a bet. The change had nothing to do with me or my sensibilities. Lucy was just working on the essay.

That winter Lucy spent eight weeks at the MacDowell colony in New Hampshire. My residency there had ended the week before hers began and I left my cross-country skis behind for her because the snow had been especially good that year. All she had to do was write her book proposal, twenty pages, this time on aspects of love, but she was sidetracked by the pool table. The coolest people there played pool and she spent her afternoons perfecting her game. She came back to New York eight weeks later without having written a single page, bought herself a professional pool cue that screwed apart and fit into a case that looked like it carried a piccolo, and started hanging out in pool halls. "I did manage to have sex on the pool table," she said.

What is easy for one person is impossible for another. I thought the easy money was in magazine articles and the sensible living was in writing books, but those were the things that made Lucy feel positively tortured. She told me she was taking a teaching job.

"It's too much work!" I said. Teaching absolutely used me up and turned me out as empty as a candy wrapper.

"I need the structure," Lucy said. "It will force me to organize my time. I don't think all this free time is good for me."

She was right, of course. She had taught before and she liked a routine and she liked having people around, two things I never went in for. In the years that followed, Lucy taught at Sarah Lawrence. She taught at the New School. She taught at Bennington and Amherst and occasionally ran a private class in her apartment for which she charged good money. She taught in a low-residency graduate program where the student work was mailed to her in packets and then twice a year she met her students for intensive classes. Some semesters she taught at three different places at once. She taught in summer workshops. She taught for ten weeks in Montana. She flew all over the country giving guest lectures and three-day workshops. She was a huge favorite among high school students and she was forever flying off to some well-heeled prep school that paid her a bundle to stand on a stage and be herself for an hour while the students cheered her as if she were Elvis. In short, she worked. She could mark up student papers for hours without so much as getting up for a glass of water. She helped write a draft of Monty Roberts's book, *The Man Who Whispered to Horses*. She spent countless hours listening to his stories and going over his notes. She could make herself write when it was his story she was telling. The publisher said they were happy with her work, but in the end Roberts rejected it, and so she didn't get the second half of her advance. Once again Lucy tried to turn herself back to her own writing.

"I'm declaring a State of Emergency," she said to me over the phone.

"Meaning?"

"Six pages a day, and I can't leave the house unless it's to go to the Writer's Room, and I can't answer the phone until I've written my pages. No going to the gym. No going out at night." The Writer's Room was a place not too far from her apartment where she had a desk that was only a few feet away from other writers who needed a place to go and work. Her apartment had the bad habit of becoming too lonely after a while.

"Lucy."

"Okay, maybe some going out at night. But only if I've written six pages. I'll only go out if I write a bonus page."

The State of Emergency lifted and lowered like a fog until I couldn't quite tell if we were in one or not. She took my phone calls either way. Lucy looked at writing the way other people thought about diets, except that she was always pulling for her numbers to go up while everyone else was trying to get their numbers down. She used the State of Emergency for essays she had promised to anthologies and magazines. Writing was always something that was owed, always overdue.

*        *        *

Then, in January of 1998, Lucy did write a twenty-page proposal, and her agent sold it to an editor at Doubleday who Lucy had never worked with before for a very healthy advance. She had decided to write a novel.

"You'll have to help me with the plot," she said. "The whole plot thing seems like it would be tricky."

"I'm sure you can manage a plot, but why not just write it as non-fiction? Wouldn't that be so much easier?" The story was about a woman with a mysterious older brother. The brother leaves home early and disappears from her life, abandoning her to the task of dealing with their difficult parents. When the parents die, she sets off on a quest to find him. It was not too far a stretch from the story of her brother, Sean, who had died in 1991, years and years after Lucy had last spoken to him.

"It's a novel," she said.

"Then it's a novel. Just let me help you, let me read it. We can talk about it." Lucy and I talked on the phone almost every day, and flew back and forth between Nashville and New York for regular visits, but we hardly ever talked about writing. We talked about not writing, or writing that was due, but whenever I asked Lucy if she wanted to exchange pages with me, she wasn't interested and I didn't push the point. I knew that by writing a novel, she felt like she was straying onto my turf. For Lucy it was very important that our professional careers remain separate. When I had wanted to work with her editor, Betsy Lerner, for my third novel, *The Magician's Assistant,* Lucy gave me her grudging approval. But after I met with Betsy and told Lucy how much I liked her and how I hoped she'd buy the book, Lucy changed her mind and told me I wasn't allowed to work with Betsy after all.

Sitting on her couch in SoHo wearing my most professional-looking outfit, feeling like a complete idiot, I said, "But I asked you. You told me I could." What I didn't say is, Why am I asking for your permission in the first place?

Lucy just shrugged. "I changed my mind."

There were plenty of people in the world writing novels. It was in no way something I imagined myself to own. But I was the ant, and the thought of Lucy taking so much money for something she didn't know how to do filled me with panic. It was my panic though, not hers, so I kept it to myself.

The early flush of the Doubleday contract was a good one. Lucy had money again, and what's more, she had a plan. After years of failing to come up with a proposal, she had finally been successful. She made deals with herself about the organization of her time. She was still teaching at two schools, but now she was determined to carve out regular hours for writing. Lucy and her friend Joy swore to e-mail each other a certain number of pages every week that they also swore never to read. In doing this they had the obligation without the judgment. Whoever failed to meet their weekly quota was committed to clean the other's bathroom.

One day I called Lucy and she told me she had written well all morning and was feeling good about life on earth.

"Read me what you've got," I said.

"Someday I will."

"No, today, now." I brought the phone over to the sofa in my study and pushed off my shoes. "There," I said. "I'm lying down. Read to me."

And so she did, and I closed my eyes. She read a scene in which the narrator worked as a translator in a hospital, and how she came home to find a spiderweb in her kitchen.

"That's enough," she said.

"Not enough. Keep reading."

The part about the spiderweb was very long and very beautiful and I thought about Lucy as a girl at Sarah Lawrence, reading her poems at the coffee shop, and Lucy at Iowa the night she read at Prairie Lights Bookstore, and in that spider's web were the poems she wrote out by hand in the surgical ward in Aberdeen and sent to me in thin blue envelopes. Her writing was beautiful and compelling and every time she said that was all, I told her more, and she read more.

"You're a poet," I said when she read me everything she had.

"I want to be a novelist."

"You're a novelist, too. Don't worry about that." I believed at that moment there was nothing to worry about. Her writing was gorgeous. She could write a novel as long as she could find a way to stay in her chair.

Chapter Thirteen

"I WAS TALKING TO A WOMAN I KNOW," LUCY SAID TO ME, "and she has a really great husband and she loves him and they have a great kid. They have what seems to be a perfect family. It's her idea of a perfect family, but she says she can't enjoy it because she's so unhappy about her writing. She can't get anything published and she hates her job. She works in an office and it's boring. She was saying that I was so lucky because my career was going well, like that was the only thing that mattered. And then I thought, remember when I used to want to be a writer so badly? I forget about that all the time. I think it's been this way forever, but I used to be so worried I wasn't going to make it. I wonder if I had found the perfect man and fallen in love but had never been able to get anything published, would I be just as miserable as I am now?"

The question of love was a dark hole into which Lucy swam daily. She claimed to be alone, alone, alone, and bringing up the legions of friends who adored her was only an irritant. "It's not the same," she said pointedly, as if she was being given an apple when what she had asked for was a pony. She was also not interested in having you point out the fact that she had more sex than all of her close friends combined and that often it was, by her own accounts, really good sex. She had also had two serious, longterm relationships since she had moved to the city from

Provincetown, one with Stephen and then later with Andy. All of her friends liked both of these men. We liked that Lucy wasn't so lonely when she was with them. But she said in both cases the relationships were too flawed. Stephen was a painter who worked construction, made little money, and didn't think about the future. Andy was a painter who was often frustrated by trying to balance his art and his successful cabinetry business. Lucy felt that he was more interested in talking about his problems than hers. She believed that both of them were ultimately holding her up from meeting the better men who were out there.

"Who has a perfect relationship?" I said to her on the phone one night. "It's always going to be something. It's just a matter of whether or not you're going to stick it out and work on it." She wanted to break up with Andy. She had long since broken up with Stephen but he was often around and a reconciliation wasn't out of the question. I was extremely fond of Stephen, who was a real sweetheart of a guy, but I wanted Lucy to stay with Andy. Andy drove her crazy, and she could be viciously unkind to him, but the very fact that he struggled with problems of his own forced her at times to assume the role of the responsible party, and that was good for her. Andy was incredibly loyal to Lucy and made heroic efforts to help and protect her. Even though she was often exasperated, she was also happier and less depressed with Andy than I had ever known her to be. He was romantic. He paid attention to details. He had a fine intelligence and she respected him as an artist. When things were going right between the two of them, they spoke of getting married. I figured if the formula worked, no matter why it worked, she was better off sticking with it.

But Lucy had been alone too much of her life, and in her loneliness she had constructed a vision of what a perfect relationship would look like. Love, in her imagination, was so dazzling, so tender and unconditional, that anything human seemed impossibly thin by comparison.

Lucy's loneliness was breathtaking in its enormity. If she emptied out Grand Central Station and filled it with the people she knew well, the people who loved her, there would be more than a hundred people there. But a hundred people in such a huge space just rattle around. You could squeeze us all into a single bar. With some effort you could push us into a magazine shop. If you added to that number all the people who loved her because of her book, all the people who admired her, all the people who had heard her speak or had seen her on television or listened to her on the radio and loved the sound of her odd little voice, you could pack in thousands and thousands more people, and still it wouldn't feel full, not full enough to take up every square inch of her loneliness. Lucy thought that all she needed was one person, the right person, and all the empty space would be taken away from her. But there was no one in the world who was big enough for that. She believed that if she had a jaw that was like everyone else's jaw, she would have found that person by now. She was trapped in a room full of mirrors, and every direction she looked in she saw herself, her face, her loneliness. She couldn't see that no one else was perfect either, and that so much of love was the work of it. She had worked on everything else. Love would have to be charmed.

When she was alone again, she decided to be proactive. She would not be one of those women who sat in her apartment feeling miserable without trying to do anything about it. She took on being single the same way she'd taken on being a writer when she was sick in Aberdeen, with action and tenacity. She would go out. She would meet men. She placed an ad in the *New York Review of Books,* a place where a friend of hers had found true and intellectual love. She listed herself as a successful author who was not interested in dating other authors. As for her physical appearance, she said that she was "fetching." The letters came in and she went on several dates with mixed results. One guy was bad in bed, another had a very hairy back. Then she got a letter from George Stephanopoulos.

"What!"

She read me the note, which said he might be disqualified because he had written a book (which he did not mention was currently on the *New York Times* best-seller list) but that he was not primarily a writer. He said he had been intrigued by the word *fetching*. It wasn't a word you saw much anymore. "It's on a note card that has *George Stephanopoulos* embossed on the top. It's a nice piece of stationery."

"I'm speechless."

"But what if it's a hoax? What if someone I know is playing a trick on me?"

"That would be kind of an elaborate trick, to have stationery printed up."

"Who would have thought that George Stephanopoulos read the personal ads?"

"Who would have thought he answered them?"

"You can't just say George," Lucy said. "There really is no point. You have to say George Stephanopoulos."

She was right, and so we said the name over and over again.

George Stephanopoulos was teaching that semester at Columbia and so was living in New York. When Lucy called his number and got his voice mail, she again considered that someone might be playing an extremely ambitious trick, but when he returned the call and she saw 'G. Stephanopoulos' pop up on caller ID, she finally had the hard proof she needed that he had answered her ad. He was funny on the phone and seemed smart and slightly, appropriately, nervous. They made a date.

It was the summer of 1999. John Kennedy Jr. was married, paving the way for George Stephanopoulos to be the most eligible bachelor in the Democratic Party, and Lucy was meeting him for drinks. I was on my way to Provincetown to teach again in the summer program and she wanted me to swing by New York on the way to help her decide what to wear. I was only too happy to oblige. The truth was, even though I was in a fine relationship of my own, I envied Lucy her date. All her friends did, and that was the thing that made it so wonderful for her. She wanted to be envied. She wanted to go out with someone who wasn't available to the rest of us. No one was more excited about all of this than Karl, who was a big fan of both Stephanopoulos and Lucy. He got on the phone and begged her to let us get a table on the other side of the restaurant where we could watch. "I promise we won't say a word," he said. She told him no.

In the end we decided on a silvery raw silk cocktail dress that was very Grace Kelly: fitted in the waist, a full skirt, and showed off her pretty arms. It was too dressy for any other blind date in the world but for this one it seemed completely appropriate.

"I don't think he's going to fall in love with me," she said. "So if I only get to meet him once, I want to look good."

I met up with Karl in Provincetown and on the night of the date we walked around with his cellphone, waiting for reports. She called once on her way to the bar, once from the restroom (but the reception was very poor) and a third time when she got home.

"He's a very nice guy," she said in the same tone she might have used at the end of any blind date. "Very smart. We had a great talk about politics."

"And?"

"He's cute, but definitely no sparks. It just wasn't there. I'd love to be friends with him, though. He'd be a great person to talk to."

"Mutually no sparks?" I was on the street in Provincetown at ten o'clock on a summer night and it was nearly impossible to find a quiet space behind a tree. Every sentence Lucy said, Karl wanted me to repeat.

"No sparks all around," she said.

LUCY WAS QUITE good at keeping other people's secrets, but she was lousy with her own. She had decided that it would be the gentlemanly thing to do not to mention the date since no one had fallen in love, but the problem was before she had gone out with him she had told everyone in the world, so now she was forever taking people aside and whispering over the details. "But don't tell," she would end the story every time.

"I went to a party sworn to secrecy about Lucy's date," our friend Artie told me, "and then when I got there every single person told me in confidence that Lucy had gone out with George Stephanopoulos."

That was the payoff for the date—not love, but the right to confide the experience and see the disbelief and then the thrill played out over and over again. It was a good story until the night she told it at a party to a group of people and an unpleasant writer we knew said, "Well, did you tell him about your face when you made the date? He did know about your face before, right?" And after that it wasn't a good story at all. Lucy, breathless, left the room. She said she felt like she had been punched. Of course that must have been the thing that everyone was thinking, everyone she told the story to. Did you tell him about your face?

After that she asked me constantly, "Why didn't he call me again?"

"You said that he wouldn't. You said mutually no sparks."

"It's because I'm ugly," she said. "I know why."

\*       \*       \*

YEARS BEFORE she wrote from Scotland,

*Dearest Axiom of Faith,*

*Your letters always have the most pronounced effect on me, it's really incredible. I'll admit I was feeling a little sorry for myself, my box has been empty so often, but your letter came today and changed everything around. I wonder if this is a little stupid on my part, but never mind that, I won't ponder that just now.[. . .]*

*I've been thinking, Ann, I seriously think you ought to go "play the field" a little. Unless I'm wrong, it seems to me that all your relation-ships have been real heavy-duty type ones: I really do believe that you should go out and learn that there are, as Leonard Cohen sings, "many sweet companions, many satisfying one night stands." There aren't really, of course; all relationships cause trouble of one sort sooner or later, but there is this level in which you can be with people and it can be sweet and nice and temporary. I mean, hey, you're young, you're a looker, and you've got (believe it or not), a sensible little head screwed onto your shoulders. It's funny—I think for me it's time I finally had a serious sort of relationship, and here I am advising you to go out and sew your oats. Maybe it's little inconsistencies like this that make our friendship work so well. And I don't know, maybe this is really bad advice for you, maybe you want to be loyal, maybe you don't think it's right to "use" men in the first place—but think about it, if only so as to reaffirm all the reasons why you wouldn't. For me, I always wonder what would have happened to me, to my way of thinking about sex, if I'd never met B——. I think he brought out the user in me, the part that is willing to use men purely and simply for my own ends, which is ulti-mately perverted as my end is to feel less lonely, and for all the men I've had, I've never felt lonelier. Shit, that word comes up a lot, doesn't it? (In all the various spellings I give it.)*

*Okay, it's Sunday now, and I've been giving serious consideration to giving you a call. It's late in the afternoon and I've just been dawdling about all day, feeling a bit useless, and came back here determined to write, yet somehow seem to have gone back to this letter instead. I've been thinking about how writing, for me, is an intense mixture of self-hatred and self-love. I went to see Mr. Fenton, my surgeon, yesterday, and he was very kind, very apologetic that it's all taking so long. Of course, it's best to take one's time, but it is all turning into real palaver. Things are much improved appearance wise since my last op five weeks ago (or so), but it will be three more months before he can do anything major appearance wise again. In the meantime I'll go in "shortly" (I guess next week or the week after) for a little work neatening up the left side. Sort of an appeasement operation, I think, something to keep me busy. In the meantime, there are a few things going through my head. One, that I'm a bloody lazy pig and should get a job instead of sponging off the government, and two, that as my face gets closer and closer to completion, I'm going to have to start dealing with disappointment, with the reality that I will never be beautiful—something I could always dream of when there were still so many operations to go. In truth, I'm pretty average, perhaps a bit less so because of the scars and all. I look at myself in the mirror at least a hundred times a day (maybe I should stop this), trying to figure out what I look like, and I can't. I have absolutely zero idea of how I'm perceived by joe butterscotch on the street. Sleeping with this D-guy did help, but it did some damage as well. I feel sort of like I should talk to a psychologist or something about it, but they don't do stuff like that here, there is no local friendly community health center; you have to ask your GP, who'd send you round the local loony bin for a consultation, and since they're really big on drugs here, you'd probably just walk out with a prescription. I guess what I have to do is*

*write, work out, and pray for something to happen next year, something*
*good.*

For a while Lucy saw a psychiatrist named Ellen who encouraged
her to limit talking about her sadness to her twice-weekly office visits.
"I'm not going to talk about being lonely or depressed," Lucy said.
"I'm not going to ask my friends if they love me or if I'll ever have sex
again. I'm not going to talk about being ugly. All of that I save for her."

"So how do you feel?"

"I feel pretty good," she said tentatively, "but I have to wonder if it
isn't a false kind of feeling good."

Lucy did seem happier to me when she was with Ellen, but maybe it
was just wishful thinking on my part. I've always been a believer in
repression.

Lucy's next psychiatrist was Joe. While Ellen might have had a
point and possibly even made Lucy feel better, it was Joe whom she
loved, and Joe, from her reports, was extremely impressed by Lucy. She
said she was enjoying a full-blown transference. It was important to
Lucy that she was the favorite patient, the most fascinating case, and
once again she was. When she was running perilously low on money
again, Joe proved his devotion by cutting his rate while adding on an
extra session as well.

Not only was she the most fascinating case psychologically, she still
posed a physical challenge. She was choking more and more often and
having regular bouts of pneumonia. She went to NYU Medical Center
and had a swallowing survey done that showed that ten percent of
everything she ate or drank went into her lungs. Lucy's lips no longer
came together unless she used her fingers to hold them, and this inability to create an oral seal was the main cause of the swallowing prob-

lems. It also meant she had problems kissing, which drove her crazy. She could open her mouth a smaller and then smaller amount, and she was having more facial pain. The grafts that had been done so successfully in Scotland had begun to reabsorb and bit by bit, the lower half of her face was shrinking again. She also continued to hold on to the dream of getting teeth so that she could eat more easily. Lucy's weight hovered around 100 pounds and she seemed to live on mashed potatoes and cans of Ensure.

A few days after the swallowing survey, Karl and I came to New York to go to the opera. I bought three tickets for both nights. Lucy and I had taken in a lot of opera together over the years. She did an extremely impressive imitation of the Queen of the Night and was always trilling as we walked past the fountain at Lincoln Center. But this time she was depressed and wouldn't sing. It was March and freezing and Lucy looked nearly lost inside her big leather jacket. Before *Tosca*, we had dinner at Mr. Chow's and she talked to Karl about her medical options. She wanted him to explain the survey in a way that the doctors hadn't had the time for. It was early and we more or less had the restaurant to ourselves. When the food came, she couldn't eat any of it. Everything we'd ordered had turned out to be too spicy or too chewy. We said we'd be glad to go someplace else, but Lucy shook it off and ordered another drink. Her eyes were damp and red and she wiped at them with her fingers. "I'm just so tired," she said. "I'm not sleeping."

Lucy had recently gone on antidepressants, but every one she tried kept her up, and then she tried sleeping pills. "It's a work in progress," she said.

After the opera Karl went back to the hotel and Lucy and I went for drinks at a bar near Lincoln Center. We had been there once before with my mother when the three of us had gone to see *La Bohème*. Lucy had asked for a glass of sherry. The bartender brought my mother and me our drinks and then set down a plate of strawberries and blueberries in front of Lucy.

We looked at the fruit, completely unable to make the connection, and then it dawned on us. "Sherry," she said. "Not berries."

The bartender, never looking at her, whisked up the plate and set it in front of a pretty girl sitting alone on the other side of the bar. He leaned over and whispered something to her, which made her laugh. A minute later he came back holding another plate. "For you," he said. He set down a plate of maraschino cherries in front of Lucy.

"SHERRY!" she said.

He looked at her as if she had just wandered in from Uzbekistan and demanded a goat.

"SHERRY!" I said, ready to tear him apart. "It's a DRINK. Give her a glass of sherry."

"There is no such thing," the bartender said, and turned away.

Now we laughed about the sherry-berry-cherry story, and then when we were finished laughing Lucy told me how badly things were going. She was lonely, she wasn't writing, and she couldn't bear living without teeth anymore.

"I'm going to have a fund-raiser for my teeth," she said. "I'm going to call it Let Her Eat Steak."

"I could get people to sponsor individual teeth. For $1,500 you could be a tooth fairy. Between the two of us, we could come up with a whole mouthful. We could even get tiny donor plaques to attach at the gum line. 'This tooth is brought to you through the generous contributions of Ann Patchett and Karl VanDevender.'"

"A little plaque on my teeth?" Lucy said.

Even though we could come up with ways to get the money, the implants were still unobtainable. The plastic surgeon Lucy saw in

Nashville was right; there simply wasn't enough bone to sink them into. She had started talking to other surgeons, all of whom had completely different ideas about how to tackle the project. The idea she'd heard that seemed most promising was to remove the fibula from her leg and graft it into the jaw. Lucy told me this and then took down a glass of Jack Daniel's in one unbearable swallow that made her choke and weep all over again. Lucy really couldn't tolerate alcohol and so she always gulped instead of sipped. She made the nicest drink look like she had accidentally downed a glass of insect repellent, then ordered another.

Once she stopped coughing, I asked her, "So the idea is you'll be able to chew but not walk?"

"That's what I thought, but it turns out that the fibula is the appendix of the skeletal system. It's really doing next to nothing down there."

"I don't know, pet, that sounds a little too abusive to me."

But the plan was even more abusive than I thought. The first surgery was to remove the bone from her leg and then graft it into her face. After six or eight months there would be a second surgery in which a series of external bolts would be placed on her jaw that would be tightened regularly over a period of several months, thus melding the implant to the native bone. ("I'll have a little key," she explained. "Like roller skates.") Finally there would be a third surgery where the bolts would be removed and some shaping would be done, and maybe there would be a fourth, just a small one for touch-ups. Lucy reported this in her normal, cavalier way, but I felt absolutely weak. I took a long pull off my own drink and closed my eyes. "There has to be another way."

"There's not."

That night I kissed her in the cold rain and put her in a cab. I would see her again the next night for *Porgy and Bess,* but in between I wouldn't sleep. I stayed up worrying about Lucy, something I had long ago promised myself not to do.

After I was home, Lucy talked to Mr. Fenton in Scotland, who was also not in favor of the surgery. He thought it was too new, and there were no studies about how people managed without their fibulas long-term. He thought it was possible she could eventually wind up crippled.

"He's in Scotland," she said. "They're just behind."

Why did I feel like I was trying to talk Lucy out of dating a dangerous man? The whole thing had such a romantic coloring to it and now that she had decided to place her trust in these surgeons (it took two to do such a procedure), there was nothing that could dissuade her.

"At least wait until you've finished your novel," I said. "I just have a terrible feeling that this whole thing is one spectacular stall from working."

"I have to have the surgery."

"I understand that you have to have surgery, but if you do it now or a year from now it's not going to make a huge difference. Once you write the book you'll have money again, you'll have your career back on track, you won't have to worry about owing anything to anyone. The book will bring all sorts of new people into your life. There are a set of problems that will be corrected by surgery, but there's an even bigger set of problems that are going to be solved by finishing the book." I never lost sight of how much Lucy loved her fame and I thought that if it could come back to her full force, some of the happiness would return as well.

"I can't wait another year for the surgery. These will be the last surgeries I ever have to have and I need to be finished with them. I've got to put this behind me so I can get on with my life. I'm not going to be forty and still having surgery."

In *Autobiography of a Face,* Lucy talked about how she spent her childhood thinking that real life would start after the surgeries stopped. I thought she was being ironic this time, dredging up an idea she'd relied on for so many years. There was no irony.

We kept going around about it but I wasn't going to talk her into waiting any more than I'd ever been able to talk her into anything else. Her book was overdue and the advance money was long gone. There had been some rumblings that her contract could be canceled, but she told her editor she needed an extension for medical reasons and she got one. The surgery was scheduled for the end of June, 2000.

EVEN IN THE BEST of times, Lucy wasn't so good about opening the mail. Like the phone, it was a constant reminder that she was in debt, behind, pursued. But when she got depressed, she gave up on it altogether. She kept a giant Hefty bag by her front door and when she walked in, she simply threw the contents of her mailbox into the trash bag. It wasn't trash exactly—she didn't throw it out—but she kept it there as a reminder of everything that was wrong. She had moved to a beautiful little apartment in the National Arts Club on Gramercy Park the year before and now picked up her mail from the large boxes behind the front desk as if nothing was wrong at all, but in her apartment the ever-growing bag plagued her.

"Send it to me," I said one day not long after I had seen her. She had been telling me about how depressed the bag was making her.

"I can't send you my mail," she said.

"Hang up the phone, walk to one of those mailbox stores, and send it to me. Don't look in the bag, don't think about it, just do it."

"I'm too embarrassed."

"Look, pet, you have a lot of terrible problems I can't help you with, but at least I can do this." I could feel myself starting to worry and I needed something tangible to do.

Lucy sprung for Federal Express and so the box came the next day. I have to say, it was larger and more terrifying than I had expected. When I turned it over on the floor of my apartment, it made an avalanche of unopened white envelopes, hundreds of letters sliding over each other like uniform flounder, each demanding attention and reply. The very sight of them depressed me and I tried to imagine how much more depressing they would have been were they actually mine. I got a knife and started to open them one by one, throwing the envelopes away, putting everything into stacks, trying to bring order to chaos. Once everything was spread out in front of me, I found that it wasn't really as bad as either of us thought. These weren't hundreds of new bills, they were hundreds of dunning notices for the same handful of bills. Lucy, thank God, was never able to get a credit card because of her unpaid student loans, and she had her regular phone and cellphone bills taken directly out of her checking account. Sometimes a twenty-dollar charge from a doctor had twenty repeat notices. For a few thousand dollars, I was able to pay off all of it except the student loans and federal taxes. I forged her name on a couple of overdue publishing contracts and typed up polite thank-you notes for fan letters and forged her name on those as well. I paid off the swallowing survey.

A lovely thing about Lucy was that she responded so well to practical assistance. It really did cheer her up. We talked for an hour that night and laughed about what had really been inside those envelopes. It was like having a bad dream in the night in which a parent comes and flips on the light in the bedroom to show you that there was never really anything under the bed that was planning to eat you alive.

## Chapter Fourteen

IN THE FALL OF 1999, AT THE AGE OF THIRTY-FIVE, I
got a bad case of chicken pox, which was itself a fairly minor medical calamity, but those chicken pox, for no reason anyone could figure
out, tripped me into a case of hives that stayed with me on and off for a
year and a half. Unlike the chicken pox, the hives were a disaster. Every
day I would wake up in a reconfigured body. Some mornings my back
would be a solid red welt, and then slowly over the course of the day
the welt would break into individual lumps that would march in a
clockwise circle and take over my chest. Some days my right eye would
be swollen shut, and then the left, and on days with no luck it was the
right and the left. My lips turned inside out if I so much as knocked
against them with my toothbrush. Then the hives would leave my face
for a while and go into my joints, swelling my ankles up to hot grape-
fruits until I couldn't pull on any of my shoes, or they would get into
my wrists and I couldn't write.

"You should set up a camera on a tripod," Lucy said, "and then
every day at the same time take off all your clothes and take your picture, front and back."

It was a good idea, but I was unwilling to believe that they would
ever stick around so long or so dramatically. If I had known, I would
have taken her advice and bought a camera.

In June of 2000 I took my hot, itchy, lumpy self to New York. My plan was to spend a few days with Lucy and help her get everything organized before the surgery, then I would go to Provincetown to teach for a week, then I would come back and help take care of Lucy after the surgery. Lucy wanted to purge her apartment, thinking that once she had a bone taken out of her leg, it wouldn't be the time to start dragging trash bags down the hall.

"I have a sudden mad desire for order," she said.

"And we all know who to call when the urge for order strikes."

We worked for days, going through stacks of papers and file drawers. We took every last thing out of her closet and I made her try on her clothes and look in the mirror and tell me if she ever planned to wear the outfit again. There was the navy tunic from the *Today* show, all of her riding boots, a half dozen pairs of jeans, a never-ending parade of thrift-store cocktail dresses and a few dresses from Prada, purchased when the cash was running high, all knotted up together on the floor of her closet. We went through her books, which were stacked on top of each other, stacked on the floor in front of the bookshelves, stacked perilously high on the tiny bookshelf behind the toilet. We boxed away the ones she never planned to read and the ones she liked but would never want to read again and the ones she didn't like. She found a used bookstore that was willing to make pickups. An accurate reading list compiled from her floor would tell half the story of her life. She had read every word of Tolstoy and Dostoevsky and Chekhov, Nabokov and Marquez and Mann. They were still there, scattered in with *Das Kapital* and *Calculus Made Easy* and *The Freud Reader* and a book of Lucian Freud's paintings. The narrow space around her mattress in her sleeping loft was crowded with Heidegger and Derrida, Debord and Foucault. *Postmodernism; or, The Cultural Logic of Late Capitalism* was beneath her copy of *The Matrix*. There were musty thrift-store hardbacks, William Maxwell's *They Came Like Swallows*, and something called *The Last of the Peshaws: A Tale of the Third Maratha War*. The old book on French cinema was beside a tape of *Groundhog Day*. There was a stack of "Idiot Guides": *The Complete Idiot's Guide to Buddhism, The Complete Idiot's Guide to Tantric Sex, The Complete Idiot's Guide to Learning Italian*.

"Why do you buy these things?" I said, tossing them off to the discard pile.

She pulled them out again. "I *like* them."

We dusted the books off, separated the good from the impossible, and boxed. She was happy to get rid of novels, even good novels, because she wouldn't read them again, but she wouldn't go through the poetry. "It's bad luck to throw a poetry book away," she said.

We went through the CDs and found six copies of *Ambient 1: Music for Airports* ("I always think I've lost it," she said). I had the supreme pleasure of putting all the discs back in their correct cases. When we had the place scrubbed down and reassembled and had dragged the last giant bag of trash away, we took showers and went for sushi. We were victorious, featherlight, blissful in our exhaustion. Lucy and I did the twist on the sidewalk waiting for the Walk sign to turn green. I think I felt more relieved by the cleaning than she did. I know I was more worried about the impending trip to the hospital. I was leaving in the morning and when I came back, the surgery would be over.

"I've decided I'm not going to worry about finding love until all three surgeries are finished," she said. Her voice was cheerful and full of resolve. She was too thin but her arms were tan and strong. She sounded like she meant it.

"I think that's brilliant," I said.

"There's just no point wondering why someone isn't falling in love with me when I'm going to be in one state of surgical disrepair or another for the next year. I'm either going to be recovering from a surgery or getting ready for one. I'll have bolts in my face. I need to forget about love for now."

"If you could just let yourself off the hook," I said. It was the single thing I wanted most for Lucy, to have a minute of peace from her relentless desire to understand why she hadn't found True Love.

"Exactly. I'm going to have enough on my plate for a while. I don't need to beat myself up over that, too." She had talked it over with her psychiatrist and together they had come up with the plan. "Joe and I decided it's the most sensible approach."

Then God bless Joe, I thought.

"I'm going to write during my convalescence," she said. "I figure if they take a bone out of your leg, it's a good opportunity to chain yourself to the desk. Think of all the extra time I'll have if I'm not having to wonder why nobody loves me. I'll order lots of take-out and friends will come and visit me. It's all going to work out perfectly."

"It's a drastic way to get work done."

"You'll see," she said, trying to make me feel better about things. "It's all going to be great."

LUCY HAD SPENT too much of her life alone in the hospital. She checked in alone, had surgery alone, and awakened in recovery without anyone she knew to smile at her. Yet even the most impossible things become routine if you repeat them often enough. And while she had spent her life telling others not to worry, she was fine by herself, she had realized in therapy that it would be nice to have some people around; that she, in fact, expected it. She worked out an elaborate schedule of who was to visit when, and then issued an open call for people to come and see her. Lucy had her surgery on Thursday while I was still teaching in Provincetown and I returned to New York on Saturday. I had thought I would be more useful later when she was ready to come home. At home, I thought, is where she would need someone to take care of her, whereas at the hospital I would only be another visitor.

I made it to the N.Y.U. Medical Center at five o'clock on Saturday, having gone right to the airport after my final class. Lucy's friend Lucie Brock-Broido was there, as was Andy. Lucy was tiny in her hospital bed, a pale slip laid out on white sheets. She was bleary with pain and drugs but I thought she looked remarkably good. Even at this early hour I could tell her jaw was lower. Maybe I had been wrong about all of it. She wasn't bandaged or especially swollen and she cracked her eyes open a little bit, wiggled her fingers, and threw up. Lucie B-B, as she was known in the company of Lucy Grealy, was standing by with a slender suction tube and suctioned her out with the efficiency of a surgical nurse. Because Lucy could neither lift nor turn her head, it was imperative that someone be there to suction her and it clearly wasn't going to be anyone on staff. It seemed there were only two nurses on the entire floor and they raced by the room without looking in. We washed Lucy up and changed the pad beneath her shoulders, and all the while Lucie B-B made enthusiastic girl talk, as if she and Lucy were alone in a West Village coffee shop. "You look fantastic LuLuBell," she kept saying. "You are the envy of the surgical ward." Lucie B-B was a tall, slim woman, very striking, with waist-length hair. She was dressed entirely in white, as if she thought she might be able to pass herself off as a nurse instead of a poet, but the nurses were all wearing pink-and-blue scrubs.

The twenty-ninth of June fell on a Thursday that year and after the surgeons had completed their final case of the day, they swarmed from the island of Manhattan like a pack of rats, taking off for Long Island or the Cape or Bimini or wherever successful surgeons go to celebrate the independence of their country. They were absolutely, unequivocally absent. They were taking off Friday and Monday because Tuesday was the fourth, and everyone was taking off the fourth. On the Saturday of their desertion, July 1, all new surgical residents began their first rotation. It would have been difficult to find a worse calendar moment to have a bone taken out of one's leg.

Because the hospital was so radically understaffed, and because visitors were not allowed to stay past eleven-thirty, our only option was to hire a private nurse to sit with Lucy during the night to keep her from choking on her own vomit. This was her first night out of the ICU and so we made a few phone calls and wrote out our checks. I went back to Lucy's apartment and fell asleep in my clothes on her couch.

To be in New York City on a long Fourth of July weekend is to have the place to yourself. As I walked at six in the morning from Lucy's apartment to the NYU Medical Center on Thirty-first and First, I felt like I was in some postapocalyptic film: newspapers blowing through the hot, empty streets, one lone cab shooting through an endless line of open green lights, and me, pushing through the revolving glass doors.

It is too self-referential to even consider a bad case of hives when sitting at the bedside of a friend who is now wearing her fibula in her jaw, but they were there, and they were formidable, so much so that the people on the elevators pressed back against the metal walls of the box when I stepped inside. On the surgical floor, the other patients stared at me with open sympathy. There were egg-sized lumps on my arms, neck, and face. My scalp had taken on a startling topography that no amount of hair could disguise. One of my eyes (and I felt grateful that it was only one) was closed. All I was missing was a tower and a set of bells. It would have been impossible to say if I looked diseased or beaten, or which of the two scenarios would have been worse. When the rare nurse or much rarer junior doctor entered Lucy's room, their eyes scanned quickly over the girl in the bed and then landed on me. They appeared to be genuinely startled. "What happened?" was the first question. They already knew what had happened to Lucy.

"Hives," I said. I was getting used to them.

Lucy could go on for hours and then days about the smallest inner workings of her emotional suffering, but in the face of physical pain she was both stoic and philosophical. In her life she was in some kind of pain a great deal of the time, something she would only acknowledge if you asked her, but for the most part she didn't mention it, which was why I knew the pain she was in now was so wrenching. She laid in her bed with her eyes closed and she cried. She hadn't counted on the pain in her leg being so excruciating, but worse than that was an impossible headache. She held on to my hand and whispered over and over again, "Please make them do something."

I was ready to make them do anything. My stepfather was a surgeon and I had spent a large chunk of my youth in hospitals and in those antiseptic hallways I was fearless. As a child I had driven in from the country with him on the weekends and sat in the doctor's lounge eating doughnuts and drinking orange soda while he made rounds. If he was gone too long, I took the elevator to the obstetrics floor to look at the babies in their plastic boxes. Sometimes in the summer months he would bring me and my sister or one of my stepsisters to surgery during the week when we were bored because there was nothing else to do. My stepbrothers had only gone once and never tried it again. We would stand in the operating rooms for hours, first watching the patients flail through their intubation. Then we'd watch as another doctor neatly sliced open the skin and peeled back the useless flap of the ear and began to saw through the skull with an electric drill that made a horrible high-pitched whine and filled the room with a smoky, burning smell. We'd have to step back from the table in our oversize scrubs to avoid getting a chip of bone in our eye as it spun into the air, a small blowing geyser of snow above the patient's resting head. When all that work was finished and there was a clear hole into the brain, we were each allowed to look at it through a surgical microscope. Then my stepfather would come in and the nurses and doctors would stop telling jokes. He would reach into the brain, with the tiniest hook and knife and cut away the thing that wasn't needed. Among the children in the family, it was a contest to see who could make it all the way to the end without fainting and one by one they all hit the floor except for me. I never fainted, so every time I was allowed to go back.

Which is all to say that while I have no medical knowledge, I was not an unhandy person to bring to a hospital. I knew how to ask for things. I knew how to ask for things repeatedly, firmly, and, when it was absolutely necessary, unkindly. "My friend, who has a more complicated understanding of pain than anyone working in this hospital, says she is in pain, right now, so tell me what you're going to do." I kept track of her pills, what they were, when she got them, and in what dosage. I knew what was shot into the plastic line of her IV tube, and when she was due for another round. I could always find the nurse. And when Lucy continued to cry, I'd find her again.

I found the linen closet and made myself at home, my hive-studded feet stuck into a pair of outsize scuff slippers as I skated through the halls. I gave Lucy her baths and changed her sheets and talked a nurse into stowing the gel ice pack for her eyes in the staff's refrigerator. The nurses were nice to me. Even if I was overvigilant about Lucy's medications, I also held her up while she vomited and then cleaned her. I gave them one less patient to worry about.

At eleven o'clock in the morning the junior doctors swept into the room in a pack, all men, all white, all dully pretty in that way plastic surgery residents so often seem to be. They had never seen Lucy before and they scanned over her chart as they stood at the end of her bed, asking me about my hives.

"Miss Grealy," the young man said in a slow, loud voice that one uses with the elderly and mentally handicapped, "You Need To Be Up And Walking."

This from a doctor who didn't look old enough to order a beer in a bar.

"I can't walk," Lucy said quietly. "My leg hurts."

"The fibula isn't a weight-bearing bone," he said brightly. "Its removal will have no effect on your ability to walk. Here, does this hurt?" He pressed against the bottom of her foot with his hand and she gasped, both from the pain and the stupid unkindness of the gesture.

"Stop that," I said, and put my hand on his shoulder. I felt myself walking into a tangle of Scottish drunks on the bridge in Aberdeen. I felt again that desire to tear apart a stranger's neck with my hands. "Listen to her. She has a headache."

He took me for what I was, a woman too ugly for him to ever repair. "We'll get her some Tylenol."

"It isn't that kind of headache."

"Sometimes we can get a little headache after surgery." His voice turned loud for Lucy. "It's perfectly natural."

"I can't stand it. It isn't natural." She started to cry, even though crying in front of a doctor, even a baby doctor, broke every rule of conduct.

"She's had more surgeries than you've sat in on," I said. "If she says this is this worst headache of her life, then it is. Get her something."

He didn't answer me. He left with his party, but five minutes later the nurse came in and gave her a shot of Demerol. When she asked for another one late in the day, she got it.

The only real doctor around was Stuart Lewis, Lucy's internist, who Lucy had spoken of with great fondness. Even when he showed up in a white coat, I never had any idea if he was a doctor visiting a patient or a guy who was visiting a sick friend in the hospital. Stuart was our age, which made him ancient by the standards I had seen around the halls, and while he looked over her chart and asked a few questions about how she was feeling, what he really wanted to talk about were the Orwell essays she had loaned him. The attention seemed to pick her up as much as the Demerol and she rallied for a little conversation. I liked him because he stayed for a long time and never once took notice of my hives.

By late in the day I was barely standing. I wanted to scoot Lucy over and crawl in the bed beside her. When Lucie B-B came to relieve me at five, again dressed in white, I wanted to kiss her. She had come with all the energy I lacked, all of the positive chatter, the silly jokes. "LuLu!" she said. "You look gorgeous!" I made a mental note to myself to lighten up.

There were so many people I'd heard about for years that I got to know in the hospital. Some of them, like Lucie, I'd only met for a minute in the past, one of us going out a door while the other was coming in, but now there was plenty of time to visit. Lucy loved to see her friends together. What she wanted was for us to talk to one another and let her take in the sound of our voices without having to muster up the energy to participate. She was the unspoken center of attention, the only reason why any of us would have been there at all, except for her friend Shahid, a poet who had a brain tumor who spent a great deal of time in the neuro ICU. He waved and chatted to all the nurses who flocked into Lucy's room whenever he came by. I met Joy Nolan and Sophie Cabot-Black and Ben Taylor. I met Stephen Powers, the centerpiece of so many of Lucy's childhood stories, her oldest friend. Other people, like Nancy Green-Medea and Marion Ettlinger, were people I knew from other places and hadn't seen in ages. Her room became a sort of artists' salon. I met half the writers living in New York as they filed through with soft chocolate truffles and stuffed animals and flowers. Andy came by all the time but Lucy complained about his visits. If he talked to her, she said he was expecting her to entertain him, and if he watched television or talked to someone else, he wasn't paying enough attention to her. He was a valiant ex-boyfriend and he took the criticism in stride. He came back again the next day with flowers, and the next and the next.

For the most part we were lucky and had the room to ourselves, but for one day there was a patient with dyed red hair and a loud voice on the other side of the curtain. She was in for back surgery and was sealed into a plastic brace like a turtle in a tight shell. When she dragged herself past Lucy's bed to go to the bathroom, she would say how nice it was that some people had so many friends to take care of them, and would I be able to get her some ice and an extra blanket, which I did. On one of her passes, when Lucy was still very ill and crying quietly, the woman stopped at the foot of her bed.

"One of the nurses told me that you've had thirty-six operations," she said.

Lucy told her that was true.

"Well, I've had thirty-nine. Thirty-nine. Can you even imagine having that many?"

We simply stared at her.

"So listen to me, the voice of experience, I know it doesn't seem now like things are going to get better, but they will. When you've lived through as much as I have, you'll understand. God loves you, and He's not giving you anything more than you can handle. That's why you've got all these nice friends to take care of you."

"Okay," Lucy said, sounding exhausted. The woman waited for

more, some questions perhaps about what she had endured in her life. But none came, and so she shuffled away. I went to the nurses' station and requested a transfer to another room.

Watching Lucy in the hospital was like watching a fast-forward documentary of a little plant that pushes out of the ground, grows leaves, and then flowers, all in a matter of a minute. I carried her to the bathroom and to her chair to sit up, and then she could hobble to the chair, and then hobble to the hall holding on to me and her IV pole, and then just holding the pole, and then I would walk behind her, pushing the pole. She began to put out requests for meat loaf and mashed potatoes and flan, which poured into the hospital with all the regular guests. Soon the party at the foot of the bed was one that Lucy was attending, and the nurses came in and made us weed out our ranks. I was always the first to go. I had plenty of time with Lucy and anyway, I was grateful for the chance to walk down the street by myself and sit on a bench and try to take in everything that had happened. On the Fourth of July everyone came at night and packed into Lucy's room and we watched the fireworks slice up the darkness over the East River. Lucy's room had the most spectacular view I had ever seen.

The next day I washed her hair and scrubbed her down well, dressed her in two clean hospital gowns, and took her downstairs. We didn't ask permission (it was suspiciously easy to slip away unnoticed); we just went to the elevator and got on. The elevators at the N.Y.U. Medical Center were as packed as subway cars at rush hour and it always took a certain amount of aggressiveness to get inside, especially with a wheelchair. One of the elevators was designed for Orthodox patients and visitors and so it stopped on every single floor so that no one needed to push a button. Being on the twelfth floor, I tried to remember to avoid that one altogether.

It was hot and bright and the courtyard was filled with smokers and family members and patients who weren't so terribly sick trying to get a little sun. Lucy adored the heat and was thrilled to be out of the air conditioning. She tilted back her head as far as she could to feel the sun on her face. Everyone who passed us stopped and turned and stared with blatant curiosity, at me. Lucy couldn't stop laughing. "This is my childhood dream come true," she said. "I've just had major surgery and no one is looking at me. If only I had known to hang out with someone who had hives."

"I live to serve," I said.

When we got back to the floor, the nurses scolded us for taking the wheelchair without permission.

The next day Lucy was discharged, one week after surgery. I got her in the cab and then stashed the enormous haul from the hospital in the trunk: flowers, plants, boxes of candy, toys, along with her luggage, crutches, and the walker. When we got back to the National Arts Club, I ran all of her possessions to the desk, paid the fare, and then picked Lucy up and carried her down the long, long hallway to the elevator, and to her apartment. "Thank God it's my smallest friend who had a bone taken out of her leg," I said, panting.

"I've been training you for this for years," she said, her arms looped around my neck like a happy bride.

When I ran back downstairs to get the rest of her things the cabdriver was standing next to his car, waiting. "I wanted to make sure nobody took your stuff."

"Oh," I said, touched and a little amazed. "Thank you."

He was a dark-skinned man, Indian or Pakistani, with graying hair and sad eyes. He wasn't that much bigger than I was. "I would have carried her," he said. "You got her out too fast and I didn't know you were going to carry her all that way."

"It's okay," I said. "She doesn't weigh anything."

He looked at me and shook his head. "What kind of a woman can carry someone like that?"

I carried Lucy a lot over the next couple of days. If she walked all the way from the elevator to the sidewalk, she would be completely spent and we would have to turn right back around. Even though she could walk, her leg was in terrible pain and she was easily exhausted. So I carried her through the building and around the corner to Park Avenue. It is amazingly easy to hail a taxi with a girl in your arms. Lucy was never happier than in the moments she was held and despite everything she had been through, she was incredibly happy to be out on the street in my arms. She had several friends who could carry her. There wasn't any trick to it. She was a sparrow, a match. The trick would have been to figure out a way to do it all the time so that she could have always been happy. I carried her in and out of buildings, through rounds of doctor's appointments. Dr. Stuart gave me a handful of Claritin, which decreased the insanity of my itching for a couple of hours and then, like every other pill I had tried, never worked for me again. Lucy collected prescriptions at every stop, Percoset and Darvoset and Tylenol III with Codeine. She liked to rotate them, as one made her constipated and another one kept her up and the other did very little for the pain. After I had taken her out for undercooked pancakes, I carried her home and went to the pharmacy. They gave me everything I wanted and I put it on my credit card and nobody asked me why I wasn't Lucy Grealy or what I was doing with so many pills.

At home Lucy and I stretched out on a couch that had been unfolded into a bed and watched the video of the Talking Heads concert film *Stop Making Sense*. Those had been our favorite songs to dance to in Iowa when Lucy had been so in love with David Byrne.

"You know, I met him once," she said as he slid across the little television screen wearing a big white suit.

"You met David Byrne and you didn't tell me?"

"It was a couple of years ago, I think. There were writers and musicians reading together at Central Park and I ran into him backstage. I told him that when I was a teenager, hearing his music had saved my life. I guess it was a stupid thing to say but he was very nice about it. He was kind of shy."

"I can believe that you were famous enough to give a reading in Central Park with David Byrne, I just can't believe that you were so famous that you didn't even think to tell me about it."

Her eyes went back to the television and she bobbed her head very gently to the music. "Yeah," she said. "You'd think I would have remembered to tell you that."

When Lucy felt a little better, she went out to Connecticut to stay at her friend Stephen's horse farm and have a good, long recuperation. Sophie was coming to pick her up and drive her out to the country. I was free and tired and ready to go home, except for the fact that I wanted to keep Lucy with me, and we both cried when my luggage was packed and it was time to let go.

# Chapter Fifteen

THE PAIN IN LUCY'S LEG DID NOT ABATE. MONTHS AFTER the surgery, she was still having to stop and take a rest for every block or two she walked. The pain in her face she had accepted—that was part of the package—but her legs had been strong and dependable in a body that had often let her down. She had always gone anywhere she wanted to go without a thought. She pointed out that her left leg was slightly collapsed in the shin, and the scar bothered her. "My leg looks funny now," she said. "People are going to notice."

Who could notice a slight irregularity in a leg, I reasoned. Who would notice a scar?

As bad as she felt about her leg, Lucy was pleased with the way her face was going. The reconfiguration of her jaw had improved her speech a little, even though she still couldn't get her lips together. The doctors said that would come after the other surgeries, after the teeth. She tried not to spend too much time dwelling on herself in the mirror. Anything she saw now was just going to change. There was no sense in getting too attached to this face, or wasting time being too critical of it. The deepest part of the swelling would hang around for months, and even if that only meant a subtle change she had to remember that this was not the final product. Still, she asked about it, anyone would have asked—How do I look?

She was teaching up at Bennington and driving her Saab, a different one now, back and forth between New York and Vermont. She was trying to carve out a little time for writing but the hours were hard to find. The book was all the more overdue and she was quickly falling back into her depression.

"Why doesn't anybody love me?" she said.

"No," I said. "Wait a minute. You promised you weren't going to do that. You said that you were going to stop beating yourself up over this until all of the surgeries were over."

"I don't want to go through this alone. It's too much."

"But you *aren't* alone. You know that isn't true."

"I want a boyfriend. I'm so tired of being lonely."

"Oh, Lucy, please don't do this to yourself," I begged. "You're going to have bolts put in your face in the spring. There's so much you have to deal with. You have to finish your book. This isn't the time to wonder about love."

"You can't control these things," she said petulantly. "You can't just make a decision not to think about something. It doesn't work that way."

Sometimes when Lucy called she couldn't stop crying. Other times she called to tell me how she had cried for an entire day. "I thought I knew what it was to be depressed," she said. "But I never had any idea before this."

I always thought of how she cried in Iowa, how she would curl up in a ball on the sofa and weep and sob for hours at a time. I didn't think she had just discovered depression.

That summer I had sold my fourth novel, *Bel Canto,* and in the winter I bought my first house on the street my favorite cousins had lived on when I was growing up, three blocks away from Karl. It had never been my intention to settle in Nashville, but I had. I loved Karl, and with my mother, I shared the responsibilities of taking care of my grandmother, who was in her nineties. I wasn't going anywhere, and giving up my little one-bedroom apartment was my way of finally admitting that. I moved on the twenty-first of December and Lucy came on the twenty-third for Christmas.

In those two days, I scrambled to get the house set up. The first thing I bought was a bed for the guest room.

"Don't say guest room," Lucy said. "Say 'Lucy's Room.'"

"Lucy's room, your room, the Grealy suite."

"Much better."

Sometimes I worried that Lucy saw me as the ant I was, unglamorous, toiling. Sometimes I knew she did. Sometimes I aspired to be a grasshopper myself, to live in the city and go to parties, to have bright conversations with famous people instead of washing my grandmother's hair and making her grilled cheese sandwiches. I liked to think there was a moment in my life when I could have been a grasshopper and never thought of winter at all, but now I had a house and it wasn't even a particularly charming house with loads of character that needed fixing up. It was practical, snug, and suburban.

"I really like it," she said. "I promise you. I have another friend who was worried that I would think she had become suburban and she had, it was true. But not you, my little Angora. You just bought a nice house so that now I'll always have someplace to come home to."

"Or you could just stay," I said. "I know you don't want to live in Nashville, but you could for a while. Just step out of everything. You could get some rest, I'll make your meals, you could finish your book, save some money. For a little while it might not be such a bad idea. The guest room is bigger than your whole apartment."

"Ah," she said, raising a finger. "The what room?"

"Your room here is bigger than your whole apartment."

Lucy smiled. "I'm going to have another surgery."

"Which you could fly up for."

"And I need to see Joe and I have a job and I have my friends. I'm not going to leave New York."

I still thought she should stay with me. I had a theory about Lucy: at least some of the reason she always felt so terrible had to do with her impossibly awful diet and the fact that she never slept and drank too much. The bigger problems were beyond me to straighten out but if the little things were taken care of, the daily business of keeping the body alive, I thought that maybe the rest would have a better chance for recovery.

Most years Lucy came to Nashville for Thanksgiving or Christmas, but this year was particularly good. My mother made all of Lucy's favorite foods and we laid on the floor beneath her Christmas tree while Lucy beat on the ancient family cat, who was beside himself with joy at her return. She bought me a pair of pink pajamas covered in cowgirls and gave me a little leather-bound book full of all the doodling she had done while she was on the phone. I had often admired it in her apartment, the endless pages of curly lines and little stars. On the inside cover she had written her name, her last two addresses, and a set of dates spanning from 1996 to 2000. I thought it was incredibly sweet, but then I saw that it came with an extensive typed treatise written in an outline of what her doodling meant:

*III. How is this?*

*A. It is possible to read this "book" as a text. Leafing through it, one can see that different pages speak of different humours. Sometimes, the pages mimic what a book might actually look like (often, I find myself thinking of the 'book' written by Jack in Stanley Kubrick's film, The Shining.) Other times, the 'book' seems more visual than textual, a work similar to a drawing. Still other times, the 'book' has felt more like a performance piece, something in which the act of doing both equaled and surpassed the notion of a single moment in which a piece is 'completed.' The artist Josef Beuys once lived with a wolf in a confined space for several weeks. The only 'work' of the wolf piece was that act of conceiving the piece and then following through with the conception, so that the conceptual piece became the 'real' through an applied process which was itself invisible (i.e., the concept of the piece was the piece, rather than the instigator of a piece which then required 'work' resulting in a final, static, tangible product.)*

*b. In any event, the simple presence, here, of pages which must be leafed through consecutively, necessarily creates an active narrative, a narrative as decipherable or indecipherable as the reader may choose. All narratives, even the confusing, are implicitly hopeful; they speak of a world that can be ordered, and thus understood.*

*c. I do not know if I understand this. I think that by 'writing' in the 'book' I am engaging in the active pursuit of my non-understanding of what I am doing rather than using my lack of understanding as a reason to either avoid or be ashamed of what I am doing.*

When I finished reading it, I thought that perhaps my friend was putting a little too much energy into avoiding her novel. "So it's not just a bunch of squiggly lines you drew while you were on the phone?"

For a minute I thought Lucy was sorry she had given it to me. I loved the little book, though clearly not for the right reasons.

OUR DAYS WERE LOVELY. We went to the movies and spent time with Karl or my mother and Lucy was happy. She loved them both, and they spoiled her in different ways. My mother cooked her anything she had ever wanted to eat and sewed a new blanket for her bed, while Karl took her shopping and bought her winter coats and a fur hat. She was like the favorite daughter, celebrated and spoiled at every turn, and she basked in the attention. But in the evenings when we sat in front of the fireplace talking, it always came back to the same things: she was lonely, she was depressed, she wanted a boyfriend, she couldn't understand why no one loved her. She told me that she often had a couple of drinks and a couple of Percosets before getting in her car after midnight in Vermont and driving a hundred miles an hour over the icy back roads to New York. She said that she wanted to tempt fate.

"It's one thing to kill yourself," I said. "It's another thing entirely if you kill someone else."

"I ran my car into a tree last week and totaled it," she admitted. "I wasn't even hurt."

"Lucy," I said, "this is madness! You have to either take responsibility for yourself or admit that you can't and turn yourself over to someone else."

"Do you mean have myself committed?"

"It can't be worse than driving into trees."

But it could be worse. I remember going to visit a friend once who was locked up and when they took my purse away and locked the door behind me all I could think was, *This will never be me. This will never be me.*

"I should tell you everything."

"More," I said sadly.

"I've tried heroin a couple of times. I'm not going to do it again, but I tried it and it was pretty great."

I rested my forehead against my knees and struggled to dredge up something relevant to say. I came up empty. "You aren't some poor kid in the south Bronx with no chances and you're not some rock star who has everything in the world and I don't know who else does heroin. We're thirty-seven years old. We're too old for this."

"I'm not going to do it again."

"You're in over your head. Can I have you committed? Can I become your legal guardian? Your basic human logic?"

"I want to be better."

"I know you do, pet."

BUT NOTHING GOT BETTER. She published a collection of essays, *As Seen on T.V.*, but nothing much came of it. She was disappointed not to be reviewed in the *Times*. Lucy stayed sad, dreading the second surgery that would leave her with a set of bolts in her face for God only knew how long.

"I'm bound to get the novel finished once I have bolts in my face," she said. "Where am I going to want to go with bolts?"

She was still taking painkillers for her leg and whenever she mentioned heroin to me, it was to say she had done it for the last time and was she ever glad to get that behind her. She wanted me to come up for the bolt surgery, but I already had plans to be in California for my father's seventieth birthday. "Couldn't you schedule it for two days before or two days after?"

"It takes forever to get all these people together," she said.

"They just gave you the date. If you asked today, it might not be such a problem."

But Lucy had never asked a doctor to change his schedule and she wasn't about to start asking now. "I can't believe you aren't going to be there," she said.

"Lucy, if you can't change the date and there's not going to be anyone there, I'll ask my father to move his birthday, I really will. But if you want me there because you want everybody there, then you need to let me off the hook." If it was a test of friendship, I had already taken the test.

Joy took surgery duty. She stayed with Lucy in the OR until Lucy fell asleep and she was there when Lucy woke up. That was a very fortunate thing.

It turns out there is only one thing worse than having bolts put in your face, and that's not having bolts put in your face. When the doctors opened Lucy up, they found that the native bone was too fragile to support the procedure and that it wouldn't be possible to shape the graft from her leg as was planned. There was nothing to do, and so they closed her up. It was over.

In our friendship I had spent a lot of time telling Lucy to pull herself up, to get over the past and move on. That was my role, the best of my Catholic education in action, and I didn't worry about it because I knew that she had other friends, friends who were as close to her as I was, who were more tender. She had practical friends and emotional friends, friends with big houses to crash in and friends who were good for wild fun, and she knit us together to find the perfect balance of what she needed from all of us. But this time I couldn't do my job. This time I sat on the stairs in my father's house and I cried with her and never said that this was just a setback and we would find a way to get through it. Instead I told her the truth, that this seemed the saddest thing of all, and I didn't think there was anything to do at the moment except be sad about what had happened. She was gasping on the phone, she was crying so hard. "What am I going to do?" she asked me over and over again. I didn't know the answer.

*       *       *

I WOULD SAY that was when things fell apart, but it would imply the disassembling of a time when things were all together and I couldn't remember when that time was anymore. Lucy had started making little cuts on her hips with a razor blade. She was doing more drugs. We talked constantly about the possibility of her committing herself to a mental hospital but she kept holding it off, wanting to wait until such a time that committal sounded less painful than the life she was presently living. She kept taking drugs. Joe, her psychiatrist, kept extracting promises from her to stop this desperate behavior, telling her that if she did this or that again he would stop being her doctor. When she kept going, he stayed true to his word and dismissed her as a patient. Lucy, with a failed surgery and a bad leg, had lost the person she was sure was going to be able to save her. The only chance she had to win him back was to show him how serious she was. A little more than a month after the surgery had failed, she brought all of her bad habits together for the weekend: Percoset, drinking, cocaine, and heroin. When she called me on Monday night, it was to say that she hadn't killed herself, but not for want of trying. She couldn't get out of bed either. Lucie B-B came to her apartment and they called me at one in the morning, then at two and three-thirty, the three of us talking about what to do. Lucy couldn't stand up, but she still was afraid of committing herself.

"What is the choice, exactly?" I wanted to know.

"I could pull myself together," she said wistfully.

"I think it's much better to commit yourself than to wait until someone has you committed," Lucie B-B said from the extension in the tiny apartment. "She's going to do better if she feels like she's making the choice."

"I'd agree with that," I said. "Has anybody called Stuart?"

"You have my permission to talk about this with each other," Lucy said. "But not with anyone else."

"I'm not asking for your permission," I said.

At six o'clock in the morning, she finally made her decision. She phoned me back to say she was voluntarily committing herself. Lucie B-B called an ambulance, and the two Lucys rode to the hospital.

At seven Lucie B-B called me from the backseat of a cab speeding uptown to her apartment. She was exhausted and a little carsick. She told me Lucy was checked in. All she had to wait for was a room.

But when Lucy called collect from a pay phone at noon, it was to say she still hadn't been seen. She was sitting in the ER, still waiting for a room. It was Tuesday and she hadn't been to sleep since Thursday night. She was completely hysterical.

"Call someone to come and pick you up," I said, wondering if I could get there in time to do anything myself.

"They won't LET me leave. I signed the papers when I came in. I committed myself."

"But if you're in the emergency room, can't you just walk out the door?"

"They took my clothes. I'm in a hospital gown. They took my wallet."

"I'll call Stuart. He can get you out." It was like Alice going down the rabbit hole. All night long I had told her to commit herself and now I didn't know how to pull her out. It was a mistake, a terrible mistake.

Stuart came to the hospital, got Lucy out, and took her home on the condition that she would go and see a new psychiatrist in the morning. She agreed.

We talked every couple of hours, and for a while she slept. But every time we spoke she was worse; whatever she had in her that held things together was crumbling. When we talked the next morning, she was crying so hard she was nearly screaming. She kept having to put down the phone because she couldn't breathe.

"I can't stand this!" she said. "I can't stand this anymore." She sounded like she was being tortured. Like she was being burned.

"Are you going to the doctor?" I said.

"Why did he leave me?" She meant Joe.

"He said he couldn't help you. You're the star case. If a surgeon didn't have the skill to operate on you, then you would want him to admit that and step aside."

"But he left me!"

"Even the worst surgeon should find a better surgeon," I said. "I can come up today. I can be there in three hours."

"Wait," she said, and put down the phone again. In Nashville I listened to her cry.

Lucy went to see a new psychiatrist that morning and they called me together from her office. The two choices Lucy had were to be committed at another hospital or to place herself in the custody of a friend immediately. Could she come to Nashville right now?

I said there would be a plane ticket waiting at the airport.

An hour later I had a call from Stuart. "She really isn't well," he said.

"I know that."

"I want you to check and make sure she doesn't have any drugs with her, and I want you to not let her drink, and don't do any drugs with her." His voice was stern and serious.

I laughed, but then Stuart didn't know me. "Do you have any idea who you're talking to?" I asked.

For years I had been going to Lucy's apartment, sleeping on her sofa and pretending that I was like her. Now things were bad and she would come home to me and pretend that she lived the life of the very straight.

Whenever I'm in the Nashville airport, I am looking for Lucy. I feel my life is marked by the moments I came to meet her. When I saw her come through the gate, I thought that everything I had heard on the phone was an aberration. Nothing was so bad. Look, there she was, her arms stretched out to me. She was tiny, a spring twig in black jeans and a T-shirt, her hair cropped short and dirty, no luggage, but oh, how she flew into my arms and stayed there, holding me.

"I'm such a fuckup," she whispered in my ear.

"You're fine," I said, her tiny rib cage pressed to mine. "As long as I can keep an eye on you." Hold tight, keep her close. It was May, and so pretty that I thought by the end of the week I might be able to sell her on the charms of living in Nashville after all.

When we got in the car, I laid it out for her. I thought it was best to say whatever needed to be said while we were still in the airport parking garage so that if she couldn't bear it she'd have a way to leave. "Here's the plan," I said. "No drinking at all. No drugs, I guess that goes without saying."

"Can we smoke?"

"Absolutely. I've been thinking about starting again anyway. We'll get a pack on the way home." I leaned over in the car and took her hands. She didn't look any different. She was still Lucy, still my life. "What's happened is a big deal. It's not like breaking up with a guy. It's serious, it's medical, and I'm sure I'm out of my league in trying to help you solve what's wrong. So what I want to do is try and make you happy. I just want to have some fun, put your worries behind you for a while, you know? It's not going to solve anything, but maybe it would be good to lighten up."

Lucy lifted her eyebrows. "I think that sounds promising."

"Good. Then let's go get some doughnuts."

We went to the Krispy Kreme doughnut factory where the *Hot Doughnuts Now* sign was burning its pink neon light. From the other side of a glass window we watched the doughnuts roll down the conveyer belt and then drop into the boiling channel of oil where they bobbed, little doughy life preservers, and then were scooped up and rolled through the wall of liquid sugar. They came steadily, in a slow and orderly fashion, sailing off on a higher belt, rounding the corner out of sight. The life cycle of doughnuts was enormously comforting. We watched them for about half an hour.

"God," Lucy said with a sort of reverence, "imagine how great this would be if you were stoned."

IT TAKES A certain amount of effort to be miserable and another kind of effort to be happy, and I was willing to do the work of happiness. I figured even if I couldn't make Lucy deeply happy, I could very likely make her cheaply and immediately happy. I could provide the kind of happiness that would seem hollow if we had had the money or the time to stay in it too long. It was the same as carrying her. I couldn't do it forever, but I could do it for a while. I booked Lucy a massage and had her eyelashes dyed. I took her for a pedicure. I bought her the best pâté I could find in Nashville along with Spaghetti-O's and Hungry Jack biscuits and everything else I knew she liked. We went to a bad movie and then stayed for a second bad movie. I took her shopping and bought her whatever she wanted. And she was happy, and I was happy.

The only time I caught Lucy crying was when she would sneak off to call Joe. As soon as she heard his voice on the phone, she would start to sob.

"I don't think I can take away your telephone privileges, but I'm asking you please not to call him."

"I have to know why he left me."

"Maybe you do have to know, but not now. Just give yourself a little break. Whatever the reason is, it will still be true later."

The centerpiece of the rehabilitation was our canoe trip down the Little Harpeth River. Our plan was to figure out more of a plot for Lucy's novel, and while I paddled she sat in the front of the canoe taking notes.

It had been a dry spring and the water in the river was lower than usual for May. About every five minutes, I had to get out of the canoe and lift it off the rocky bottom to get us moving again. It was the middle of the week and we didn't see anyone else on the river that day, just the ducks, who made better time than we did, and the turtles sunning themselves on the rocks, and the snakes who held their heads out of the water like periscopes as they swam past.

"The parents were musicians," Lucy said, smoking a cigarette and staring up at the rocky cliffs on either side of our little boat. "They were lazy, self-involved, selfish. They wrote one very successful song when they were young and they lived their whole lives off that." She thought about this for a minute and then decided it wouldn't generate enough income for the kind of wretched excess she imagined for them. "They had family money, too, but they spent it on drugs. They did nothing for the children. They neglected them, abused them."

Lucy went through all the characters in detail and each one was more despicable than the one who came before. When she told me the narrator, the abandoned sister, was wildly promiscuous and drank too much and probably has sex with the character of the nephew, I suggested she ease up a little.

"We've got to have someone we care about," I said. "And it helps if that person is the one telling the story. You can write a novel in which every character is despicable later, I just think it's a bad idea for a first novel."

We came up on four fat geese standing on a shoal. They looked at us with nominal interest and then turned away. Lucy nodded. "I can see that."

But what was the family secret? What had the father left his son as an inheritance? That was the thing we tried to figure out.

"You know, pet," I said with some hesitation, "I could write it for you." I sliced my paddle in and out of the water, trying to avoid the rocks, the snakes. "We wouldn't have to tell anyone. I could write it and then you could rewrite it so that it sounded like you."

"Dear God, let's hope it never comes to that."

"But if it does. If it's putting too much pressure on you."

Lucy shuddered. In trying to come up with a new way to be helpful, I had identified the lowest point to which she could possibly sink. "It will never happen," she said.

I didn't have any better luck trying to talk her into living with me, even though this time I tried harder.

"There isn't a reason not to now. You could start seeing a new psychiatrist here. I know you don't want to stay here forever, *I* don't want to stay here forever, but for a while it would be good for you."

I wanted to keep her as much for myself as for her. We had a wonderful time that visit. Even when Lucy was devastated or difficult, she was the person I knew best in the world, the person I was the most comfortable with. Whenever I saw her, I felt like I had been living in another country, doing moderately well in another language, and then she showed up speaking English and suddenly I could speak with all the complexity and nuance that I hadn't even realized was gone. With Lucy I was a native speaker.

But Lucy was never going to live in Nashville. Even if it might have saved her life, it wasn't the life she wanted.


*Dearest Anngora, my cynical pirate of the elusive heart, my self winding watch, my showpiece, my shoelace, how are you?*

## Chapter Sixteen

My editor, Robert Jones, died of cancer in August of 2001, and I went to a small memorial service at his home in Sag Harbor a few days later. In September there was a larger service in New York and Robert's assistant, Alison Callahan, asked me along with many of the writers he had worked with, to say something about him. I loved Robert enough to think that such a task would be completely beyond me, but in the end I decided to give it a try, thinking that if I broke down there would be enough people who were crying anyway that no one would really notice. And I was right, both that I would cry and that no one would mind, and when the service was over, and the memorial reception and the memorial dinner, I went back to Lucy's, exhausted.

The television movie that had been made of my first novel years before was playing on cable and we sat in bed and watched it, cheering for the two seconds my name flashed across the screen. We both agreed that the movie was significantly worse than we had remembered.

Early the next morning, we met Adrian LeBlanc downtown at Le Gamin. Adrian and I had both put *Seventeen* long behind us. She had spent the last ten years working on the book that would be *Random Family* and now that book was close to being finished. Lucy, who was still carless since driving her Saab into a tree, had to catch the train to Vermont to teach her first class of the semester at Bennington, so she made do with one cup of coffee and a few bites of my breakfast. She kept looking at her watch.

"I really, really should go," she said. She kissed us both good-bye and was out the door. Two minutes later she was back.

"Come look at this," she said. "A plane's hit the World Trade Center."

The waiter followed Adrian and me outside, along with the handful of other diners in the restaurant. Both of the towers were on fire and we asked a woman in the street how that had happened. "The flames jumped," she said. She didn't seem alarmed. No one did. The waiter looked at us suspiciously and I promised him that we had no intention of skipping out on the check. The other patrons went back inside to eat their breakfasts.

Lucy looked at her watch. "Now I'm going to miss the train if I don't take a cab." She waved and ran off, but after we wandered back to our table she came back again. "You have to see the view of it down the street," she said. "It's amazing. Go look."

History is strangely incomprehensible when you're standing in the middle of it. Lucy, Adrian, and I all made the wrong decisions that morning but none of us could have seen it at the time. Lucy rushed on to Penn Station and made her train, which turned out to be the last train to leave New York, and Adrian and I decided to go down to the World Trade Center to see what had happened.

To say it was a beautiful day would not begin to explain it. It was that day when the end of summer intersects perfectly with the start of fall, so it was warm but the breeze was light and nearly cool. The sky would have been empty, cloudless blue, were it not for the smoke that was billowing out towards Brooklyn. While there were people on the streets looking puzzled, no one seemed to be afraid. There was a huge mass of people walking up the West Side Highway, mostly men in suits, and they were talking on their cellphones, talking to each other, their jackets hooked on a finger and slung over their shoulders. They wore sunglasses. They smiled at us. We were outside on the beautiful day, with no radio or television coverage, strolling south against a tide that was strolling north. We thought that maybe someone had had a heart attack and flown a little plane into one building, and then the fire had jumped to the other, the way we'd been told. In light of everything that happened, it seems impossible that we ever thought that, but we did. A lot of people did.

When we were about three blocks away, we stopped and tilted our chins up to watch the fire, which was the point at which I had the strangest, smallest inkling that something truly cataclysmic had happened, which was the point at which the first tower collapsed.

Lucy, locked on a train to Vermont, had a much better understanding of what was going on because she had found someone with a portable television set and was now watching everything with a voiced-over explanation. Adrian and I were running, hands locked together, with the thousands of other people who were running away from the building. We got to her apartment on Sullivan Street, climbed the five flights of stairs, and stepped out onto the fire escape, into the dream, in time to see the second tower collapse.

I couldn't leave the city and Lucy couldn't come home as the island had been shut down. Oddly, I would have been the first to admit that it was a worse deal for Lucy than it was for me. As awful as it was to be in New York, it was also, for the moment, a strange center of the world. There were no cars allowed below Fourteenth Street and people sat on their stoops and talked to one another until late in the evening while kids went down the empty streets on bicycles and roller skates wearing paper surgical masks. There were candles everywhere, and the constant acrid dust of fire. I walked to Lucy's apartment but I couldn't stay there, I couldn't sit still. I walked up to Eightieth Street and spent the night on my friend Erica's couch. All I did was walk for days, both agitated and somnambulant. I wanted to remember everything, as did Lucy, who was stuck in Vermont.

But when she managed to get back in a few nights later, she was a hellcat. Lucy, still Irish, had a virulent anti-American streak that surfaced from time to time and the wave of patriotism that had taken hold of the country and, worse yet, New York City, both revolted and enraged her. We met Stuart for dinner at an Italian restaurant around the corner from her apartment and she spoke so strongly and loudly against the sudden showing of paper flags in windows and the sentimental posters that people around the city had made (speaking of God and love and country or God and revenge and country) that I actually worried the diners at the other tables might pick her up bodily and pitch her into the street. Then I worried that I might throw her out. We got into a terrible fight over dinner, while Stuart spent most of the meal standing on the sidewalk, arguing with his ex-wife on a cellphone. I understood, as Lucy pointed out, that the United States had committed heinous acts on foreign soil throughout the world and had suffered no repercussions, but I was spending half my days reading the flyers put up by the families of the missing. That was still how people thought of them then: missing. So as for her diatribe of American evils, I didn't want to hear it. When Stuart came back looking as flustered as we were, Lucy was recounting her story about being in a bar in Vermont and how everyone was watching the news and talking about how we were going to go over there and kick some ass, just like the Bible said. She was going a million miles a minute.

"'Where does it say that we're supposed to kick ass?' I said to this guy and he said, 'In the Bible—an eye for an eye.' And I looked at all of them in this redneck bar and I said, 'Fuck the Bible!' And I left. I didn't pay for my drink."

Lucy had probably been waiting to say, "Fuck the Bible," her whole life. Now she had her moment. "You weren't here," I said in a low voice. "You went to Vermont. You don't know how it was." It was the meanest thing I could say to her, because Lucy couldn't stand the thought of being anywhere other than exactly in the middle of where everything was happening.

When we were walking home, she softened and maybe felt a little sorry for making a scene, if only because she knew I hated scenes. She twisted her arm around mine. "Don't listen to me," she said. "I just get going sometimes. You know that."

"I do."

She pushed her head into my shoulder. "And you still love me?"

I was still mad at her, furious with her, but that wasn't the question. The question was did I love her. And I always loved her.


10/15/01

*Dearest Angora,*

*How strange & sweet to be writing a card the old fashioned way. I just wanted, really, to let you know that this card represents a learning— your own relentless, good natured attempts at being a best & dear friend are rubbing off. I feel that you have in so many ways taught me— through action—what it means to be a truly great friend.*

*I just got back from Florida which turned out to be fun—actually got myself into the ocean, though I did, for the first time in my life, find myself fearful of sharks. I've also noticed a subtle re-alignment in other fears/ responses. At one point we were driving along and there were two large towers smoking. Turns out they were only huge smoke stacks, but . . . Same with loud noises. My relationship to loud noises is changed forever.*

*While in Florida I bought you a trinket, a jewelry roll-up bag, at a street vendor. I liked the thought of you traveling with all your—(my good god, I can't remember how to spell jewels (jewles? No.). Jewels. Anyway, now of course it seems like a dumb gift, and ugly, but part of learning to be a good friend is not giving into fears that are ultimately narcissistic. So here, a roll up jewelry bag: if I could fill it with its name-sake.*

*My darling pet.*

*Love, Lucy*

A month before the world fell apart, Lucy had scheduled another surgery for November 1. The same surgeons had come up with a revised plan, something that could be done in lieu of the bolts that included, among many other things, a soft tissue graft from her stomach and shortening the bone in her upper jaw. Lucy's upper jaw had never been operated on before and she thought this might be an innovative solution to her problem of closing her mouth. Again, I couldn't for the life of me understand why she wanted to go ahead with it. In Scotland she would have called it an appeasement surgery. She would have to take at least two weeks off of work. Wouldn't it be better to wait until the summer?

But I never got anywhere trying to get Lucy to wait. Now I wanted her to wait because the city seemed so unstable. Anthrax was popping up like the patternless growth of mushrooms after a storm. If something were to happen, would she want to be recovering from a soft tissue graft? Everyone I knew was set against my going back to take care of her and I stayed in a state of complete indecision as October came to an end. Lucy was sweet about it. "I understand. You don't have to come," she said. "You're totally off the hook for this one." But in that way life works, once I was off the hook it was easy to make the decision to go.

I thought it would be hard to go to New York because of the time I had spent there in September or because of the threatened dangers in the city itself, when in fact what was hard was seeing Lucy suffering. The surgery went on longer than she had anticipated and it was almost ten o'clock at night before she came down to recovery. I took the elevator to a floor marked NO VISITORS and went into doors bearing the same directive. I stood in a huge room of beds turned in every direction. It was like a dream I have all the time: I was looking for Lucy and couldn't find her. "Lucy Grealy," I said to the nurse.

"Are you family?"

I told her she was my sister. The nurse pointed to the bed I was leaning my hip against and still I couldn't find her. The person in front of me was completely unrecognizable. She looked as if someone had beaten her with a tire iron. Her head was an enormous pumpkin, every feature stretched into someone else. There was blood running out of both sides of her mouth and down her neck, blood running out of her nose. The skin over her eyes had been pulled into shimmering translucence and her breasts were bare. I was crying then, and I stood beside her and held my hand on her forehead the way she liked. Lucy often talked about how it was the most soothing gesture in the world. She wrote about it, being in the hospital as a child and having a nurse or a doctor stop to place a hand on her forehead. When the nurse, who was impossibly busy, told me that it was time for me to leave, I asked her, if she had a minute, maybe she could hold her hand on Lucy's forehead. "She likes it," I said, but the woman had already turned away. I went out into the empty hallway and sat on the floor beside a gurney and cried. Not the way I would cry, but the way she would cry. I cried myself senseless. After I left, I found out Lucy's friend Ben had come by that night and said he was her brother and stood beside her bed and held her swollen hand, and after that Joy came and said she was Lucy's sister and they let her in as well. But Lucy didn't remember any of us being there. She said later that when she woke up she was alone. All of New York felt unbearably sad and alone.

I was back at the hospital at six in the morning and though there were signs posted everywhere about when a person was allowed in the ICU and for what twenty-minute increments, I went in and pulled up a chair and no one bothered me. Lucy still looked horrible, though she was slightly more recognizable as herself. She was also still intubated from the night before, which meant she couldn't talk and could barely swallow. She was desperate to get the tube out of her nose. Her hands were swollen and tied down with IVs, but she scrawled little notes on a pad of Post-Its I had in my bag.

"You weren't there." The letters were crazy, going in every direction.

"Yes I was. You were still asleep and then they made me go out in the hall."

She motioned for me to give her back the pen. "Tube out."

"I'll ask."

I got up and talked to the nurse, who told me they couldn't do anything until the doctor came by. "It'll be soon, honey," she said to Lucy.

But when the doctor came by, one of the cowboys, he patted her ankle and said she was doing great.

"When are you going to extubate her?" I asked.

"Soon," he said and then cocked a finger at Lucy. "I'll be back soon."

"Stop saying soon," Lucy wrote. I told them.

The surgical residents came to take out the tube at eleven. It was good practice on a difficult case. They were afraid that her airway would close up and then they wouldn't be able to intubate her again. Their plan then was to drop a smaller pediatric breathing tube down inside the larger tube she had in place now and then withdraw the larger tube over it, but somehow the whole thing went wrong and she started thrashing, the wild, terrified jerking of an animal caught. They were hurting her, four of them holding her down to keep her still. I reached for her foot and a nurse kindly shoved me into the hall. When Lucy had a voice again she screamed hoarsely. Both tubes came out— the second tube had gone wrong—but her airway hadn't closed and so the residents left feeling the whole thing had been a success.

It was over and almost immediately Lucy was feeling better. I got her some ice chips and washed her face. She was tired and thirsty and sticky with the leftover adhesive of removed tape.

"You're such a good friend," she said dreamily. "What did I ever do to deserve a friend like you?"

"You're a good friend to me, too."

"Oh no I'm not. Not like you." She sighed, watching me. "But at least I can make you feel like a saint. That's what you've always wanted."

I stopped and looked at her, washcloth suspended. "That's a terrible thing to say."

Lucy shrugged barely, as much as she could move her shoulders. "It's true."

I wanted to walk away from her, go down to the commissary and drink a cup of coffee alone. I wanted to tell her that she could wait for the nurse to wash her face. "I'm not doing this for points," I said. "I'm doing this because I want to help you." I hadn't wanted to come. I would rather have been back in my own house, at my own desk working, but in her fog of morphine Lucy seemed to miss it all. She just smiled at me.

"My pet," she said.

They sent us to a step-down floor, a sort of light ICU in which a circle of beds were arranged around a nurse's desk. It was a wonderful setup, although the nurse turned me out into the hall regularly and kept the never-ending stream of visitors limited to two at a time. Lucy made progress hourly. By the next day she was off the morphine, and then she was sitting up, and then we were back to walking the halls. She had been on the table for eleven hours and she kept saying she had never felt so well after such a long surgery. No matter how bad things were for Lucy, the hospital snapped her back to her center. In the hospital she understood the rules. She knew how to behave. She also had the proof she needed that she wasn't alone, and that everybody loved her. It was my job to direct the flow of traffic, to let visitors in and pull the ones that had been there too long away to give someone else a chance. Otherwise they bottled up, chatting around the foot of her bed, happy to see one another as well as Lucy, and then the nurses would sweep through the room and send the whole lot of us away. There were so many friends, so many people who loved her, who had histories with her I had never even heard. People who were smart and funny and accomplished. So many of them. So many of us in love with her. In the evenings Joy took over, performing the same function of the alpha visitor. The only time it was ever quiet in Lucy's room was early in the morning and very late at night, and that was just the way she liked it.

"I'm going to write a book about my friends," she said to me one afternoon after dispatching Sophie and Ben for fresh magazines and a milkshake. "I have the most extraordinary friends. I've never really understood why everyone has been so good to me, and now I can interview them, talk to them and see." Then she added as a gift, "I'll write a whole chapter about you."

"I could write an entire book about you," I said, and laughed. We each could have, every visitor who filed through with their arms laden with flowers. She could have written a chapter about each of us, but we could have written a library. There could be sequels, indexes, appendixes. We would never run out of things to say.

"Do you want some time off?" I asked. "I could just stop everyone for a while so you could get some sleep."

"Oh no," Lucy said. "I want to see everybody."

I asked her how Shahid was, the poet with the brain tumor who had visited her before. I wondered if he would be coming by again. Of all the people I had met in the hospital the last time, I found him the most charming, maybe because he was so comfortable being there.

"Shahid's dying," Lucy said. "He's back with his family now. I think someone told me he was in a coma."

"I'm sorry," I said, and then added, "I liked him." I said it because I didn't know what else to say.

"Oh, Shahid was great." Lucy laughed suddenly, remembering a joke she was too tired to recount. "He was hysterical."

I stayed late that night, after all the other visitors had gone, and sat in Lucy's bed with her to watch *My Sweet Charity* on the little television. At nine o'clock Stuart came by in a lab coat. He was making rounds. He ran his finger over Lucy's incisions, read her file.

"Are you feeling pretty good now?" he said. It was a doctor's voice, not the voice of a friend who wanted to hang out and watch the end of the movie.

"I'm okay," Lucy said, not sounding okay.

"I think they'll let you out of here Wednesday, maybe Tuesday. I'll talk to the doctors." He snapped her file closed. "You get some sleep."

It was just two minutes, and he was gone. It was no longer or shorter than any of the other doctors stayed. Once the door was safely closed behind him, Lucy started to cry.

"Why doesn't he love me?" she said.

"Honey, Stuart is your friend. He's your doctor and your friend. He's not supposed to be in love with you."

"But he's single. He wants to go out with me for coffee, he wants to talk about other women, but he would never be in love with me."

"Are you in love with him?"

"I could be," she said.

"Oh, Lucy, don't do this. You really care for Stuart. He's a good friend. Don't turn it into this."

But now she was really crying, and I wanted her to settle down for fear she'd break something open. "I'm so tired of being lonely," she said.

I realized that night that there was nothing in the body I was afraid of. There was no wound I couldn't clean and dress, nothing that made me feel squeamish or ashamed. Even the pain didn't make me turn away. With the body I could be tirelessly helpful, but with her psyche, her heart, I simply froze sometimes. Past a certain point I did not know what to say. I wanted to run down the hall and find Stuart, demand that he love my friend and for that love I would give him anything he wanted in return, not that that would have been the answer or that the love could have been enough, but I would have done it just to stop her from crying. It was this suffering I couldn't stand.

*     *     *

Lucy called me at five-thirty on Sunday morning to say she wanted a bottle of apricot nectar. I asked her if this was a joke. It was not.

"At five-thirty on a Sunday?"

"It's New York," she said. "Apricot nectar is out there."

So I went off looking and the eighth place I went to, I found it. She was right in this way, there were a remarkable number of stores open, but most of them sold peach nectar or fresh orange juice or strawberry banana shakes and Lucy had made it clear she wasn't interested in substitutions. When I got there, she drank down a big glass, proclaimed it was exactly what she needed, then threw it up in a pan while I held her.

Throwing up had been a major ordeal during this surgery because she had had operations on both her stomach and her jaw. I had to sit behind her in the bed and hold her up while she vomited, my legs on either side of her hips like we were doing drills in Lamaze class. Most of the time she threw up a bright green water that looked and smelled alarmingly like Scope, some remnant of eleven hours of anesthesia.

That Sunday Lucy was getting worse. She was crying and disoriented. She had been moved into a semiprivate room and sometime during the night she had acquired a roommate who cried without stopping. She made horrible, high-pitched wails of pain and desperation that made sleep impossible and sliced through my last nerve. It was still going on, and the woman had put her television on its loudest setting to try and drown out the sound of her own suffering or trying to distract herself, but either way the din was unbearable.

"I'm so tired," Lucy cried. "I want to go home."

It was a stretch, an eleven-hour surgery on Thursday night and home on Sunday morning, but when the doctor came in, I asked him.

He was one of the surgical fellows, a tall, lanky man with a kind face who Lucy claimed to have a crush on.

"Sure," he said, looking at her over the rim of his coffee cup, "why not?"

I was hoping for something a little more medical, but I'd take it.

"I wanted to ask you about my hip," she said while she still had his attention. She pulled up her gown to show him the jagged spike of bone that a different surgeon had carved apart for a graft when we were still in college. He had left it as a dangerous, painful-looking point beneath the skin. "I wonder if it can be fixed?" she asked.

The doctor looked at it and touched it tentatively, as if to see if it were really as sharp as it appeared. "We could have fixed it this time," he said. "You should have asked. Just remember next time. It's not a problem."

His answer raised two questions: if it wasn't a problem, why had someone left it behind and no one thought to fix it for twenty years, and also, was there supposed to be a next time?

We had at least an hour before the paperwork would be ready and we could go, so I put Lucy on a plastic chair in the bathtub and washed her hair and gave her a bath, thinking we'd be better off getting it done here than trying to do it at home. When I got her all dried and dressed, I took her downstairs with her new mountain of gifts. It was considerably harder getting Lucy home this time. She should have stayed in the hospital at least another two days, and on top of that all the morning's throwing up and then the bath had exhausted her. There was a moment when we were out on the street in front of the hospital trying to get a cab that I thought I had made a terrible mistake, but we were out now and there was no going back. I carried her down the hall to the elevator, up to her apartment on the eleventh floor, and got her settled on the couch. She was too sick to leave alone and so Joy came over

to watch her while I ran to the pharmacy to have the new raft of prescriptions filled, Vicodin, Klonopin, antibiotics. I bought the pudding
cups and Ensure. When everything was settled, Lucy slept for twelve
hours. I set the alarm for every two hours to give her her pills. I kept an
elaborate chart of what she had taken and when, so that I wouldn't
forget what I had made her swallow in the middle of the night.

Because Lucy should still have been in the hospital, we had to play
hospital at home. She was sick and crying and throwing up and I was
dispensing pills and constantly calling Stuart on the phone for advice. I
carried her over to Park to hail a cab for her doctor's appointments and
every time we came back she had a prescription for more pills. I
thought she already had every narcotic known to man, but she was trying to fine-tune, find something that was better for the pain. She wasn't
pretending—the pain was formidable and the pills were all faulty in
their own ways—but what alarmed me was the sheer volume of plastic
orange bottles that were being stacked up in the apartment with no
conversations between the doctors about who was assigning what. If
she was offered a prescription for something she didn't like and had
too many, she took it anyway, just in case. The next day I took Lucy to
another doctor, who turned out to be a surgical fellow she hadn't seen
before. He gave her a prescription for eighty OxyContin.

If all of the other medications were lacking, OxyContin was the
perfect drug. Instead of slowly pulling you up towards relief, peaking,
and then sliding you down again, this pill provided a sustained and
consistent twelve-hour break from pain. It didn't make her foggy,
emotional, or sleepy. It worked beautifully and was inexpensive, which
is why it had become such a popular street drug. All you had to do to
change OxyContin into something sweeter than heroin was crush it
up. That destroyed the time-release mechanism, thus giving you twelve
hours of pain relief in one startling, beautiful minute. Eighty in the

house was like having an unreliable Rottweiler at the foot of the bed. Even the bottle was menacing, huge.

"What if I took them with me," I said casually. "I could mail them to you every week."

"You're being crazy," Lucy said.

"Then give them to Joy. Give them to Sophie. Let somebody dole them out for you. You can't keep track of so many pills."

"I've been doing this my whole life. I know how to take pills."

I went home to Tennessee and Lucy went back to Connecticut, this time to go to Sophie's farm in the country to recover. It was too soon to know if the surgery was a success, but in another week she felt significantly better. She went back to finish her class for the semester. She told me later that's when she started grinding up the OxyContin and snorting them. When they were gone, she made the simple transition back to heroin.

# Chapter Seventeen

L̲UCY HAD ALWAYS WANTED TO BE IN AA. "IT WOULD be such a great way to meet people," she said. "Plus I'd have someplace I had to go every day." She had started going to meetings at several points in her life but without any imperative, like being an alcoholic, they always wound up boring her. Meetings bored her now that she was supposed to go to Narcotics Anonymous, or they made her restless. She said there was no point in her going to AA because she wasn't about to give up drinking if she had to give up drugs. Giving up drugs meant giving up heroin. Period. No more than that.

And she did meet people, but they weren't Lou Reed or Marianne Faithful. No one was messed up in a way that was particularly romantic. One night a guy she knew from meetings called her for help, wanting to sleep in her apartment so that he wouldn't get high again, but when he showed up he was already high, and in the morning she found him shooting heroin in her kitchen. She reported the story to me over the phone the same way she might have had she woken up to find a large cockroach in her sink.

After so many years of talking to Lucy every day or every other day, I could now go weeks without hearing from her, no matter how many threatening messages I left on her answering machine. Then she would call and tell me she had been clean for three days or twenty-four hours or a week and that was it, by God, she had been down to the bottom and now she knew she would never do heroin again. These calls were usually made with laryngitis, so that I could barely understand what she was saying.

"But I thought you *were* finished." I always felt two steps behind. I was supposed to be glad she had stopped using when I didn't know she'd started up again.

"Last time I didn't really mean it," she rasped. "Even as I was telling people it was over there was this tiny part of me that knew. . . ." Her voice petered out.

"Say it again. I couldn't hear you."

"I said I knew I would still do it one more time. But this is different. This time there isn't a single part of me that wants to go back."

"How do you know it's gone?" I asked.

It was gone because she'd taken too much and passed out and vomited while she was unconscious, which accounted for her lack of voice. She was terrified of asphyxiating on her vomit, and she said she'd been careful to pass out with her head hanging over the edge of the sofa. Lucy's throat was a battleground, stripped and mined by years of surgery and intubation. Without her voice, and with the general physical misery that accompanies the aftermath of a few days of drugs, Lucy would wind up canceling her classes after a spate of using.

"Are you shooting it?"

"No!" she said. "That's disgusting. I would never do that. I only snort it." In her mind it made her a nicer brand of addict. I asked her if she had any heroin in her apartment.

"A little. Not much."

"Then don't you think it would be a good idea to get rid of it now?"

And so we would embark on the ritual of flushing whatever was left down the toilet while I listened on the phone, which I understood was a bit like listening to radio theater. Even if it was gone, it didn't matter. Her dealer delivered to her building's doorman, and his number was on the speed dial of her cellphone. She told me that at ten dollars a bag it was cheaper than pot.

Everything I knew about heroin I learned from the movies, so I thought that if she wasn't using drugs every day, she couldn't actually be addicted to them. If she could go six weeks without using, then she could quit them altogether. It wasn't as if she was out stealing television sets. But heroin seemed to be some sort of invisible leash and six weeks was as far as it would let her go. Then she was back on, then back off, feeling increasingly more miserable as the days and weeks after heroin created a vicious kind of hangover that could only be eased by heroin.

And maybe it wasn't six weeks, even if that was what she told me. Maybe it was three, maybe one.

"It inhibits your body from producing its own endorphins," she said. "At the very minute you need them the most."

"Why keep going back?" I asked. Nothing about it made sense to me.

"They don't call it heroin for nothing," she said.

Lucy was having the great love affair she had always dreamed of. It was dangerous and rocky, violently depleting, but in the few minutes that it was sweet it made her feel the all encompassing heat of love.

There would be good days, too. Days in which she called and was happy. She had been seeing a new psychiatrist, Dr. Lindy, in whom she placed great faith. She said she was finally dealing with her past. She was realizing that the enormous sadness of her life had possibly come from a source other than her face and that she had never been able to get completely well because she had always been trying to fix the wrong thing. She had talked Dr. Lindy into giving her two sessions for every one he charged, proving once again that she was the special case. I worried that maybe she wasn't strong enough to go ferreting around in the dark unhappiness of her past. But as Lucy pointed out, I was always worrying about something.

One night as I was falling sleep, Lucy called to tell me a long and complicated story about going to see her favorite blues singer Little Jimmy Scott with Andy, and how she had done heroin later that night and how Andy couldn't get a hold of her, and, thinking she might be dead or dying, called the police to break down her door. She wasn't dead, of course, just temporarily unconscious. She was furious with Andy for meddling in her business, even if what he had been trying to do was save her life. Somewhere in the middle of it all I cut her off.

"You're doing heroin again?"

"I'm not going to lie to you," she said. "I'm not going to let this drug make me into a liar like it does everyone else. I do heroin sometimes and you might as well get used to it."

"No," I said. "I'm never going to get used to it. It's never going to be conversational for me."

"Are you telling me I should lie to you?"

"I'm telling you to get off heroin," I said, and then I said good night and hung up the phone.

My old boyfriend Eli called me the next day. He was in from Rome and visiting Lucy in New York. "I'm calling on behalf of your best friend," he said lightly. "She wanted me to tell you she's a good person and you should forgive her."

"Jesus, you make it sound like I'm pissed off that she borrowed my sweater without asking," I said. But then Lucy hadn't told Eli what we were fighting about, only that I was mad at her.

\* \* \*

In February, after I hadn't heard from Lucy in a week, Joy called in the middle of the night to say that Lucy had cut her wrists, though not badly enough to need stitches, and had then taken an overdose of heroin. She was on suicide watch at Columbia Presbyterian and Lucie B-B and Sophie were on their way and she didn't think I needed to come. It was remarkably like the conversations we had around surgeries: who was taking what shift. Joy told me what Lucy had taken and I wrote it all down on a piece of scrap paper and stuck it in the kitchen drawer.

The next day I called Lucy on the pay phone in the psych ward. Joy had given me the number. It took me a half hour of trying before I got through.

"It's just like Yaddo," I said to her after someone had finally agreed to go and find her for me.

"You hate me," she said.

"I don't hate you at all. I'll be mad at you sometime when you're well, but not when you're sick. I love you."

"I'm sorry," Lucy said. "I don't do this to hurt you. I don't want to hurt you at all."

"I know that."

"I want to stop. I want to stop this and I want to get better."

"I know, darling."

"Don't stop loving me."

"I'm always going to love you."

"Don't stop taking my calls."

"Lucy," I said. "Check your answering machine sometime. I call you every day."

She should have stayed in the hospital for two weeks and I told her so. All of the friends decided she had to go to rehab and that we could pool our money and send her, but she said the timing was bad. After forty-eight hours she had convinced the doctors that she was no longer in a crisis. Without her being actively suicidal, insurance wouldn't cover the stay anymore and they discharged her into Sophie's care.

Whenever Lucy didn't call me back, I thought she was off doing drugs. "Hey, pet, it's me," I told her answering machine. "I have a terrible feeling you're high. Please call."

But she then would call the next day and say no, not high, just fine, just very busy. I always believed her, if for no other reason than I didn't know how not to.

"I went to the Writer's Room to work today," she told me over the phone. "It was the first time in ages, and there was a little sign up on the bulletin board about a girl from Sarah Lawrence who committed suicide." Lucy said her name but I didn't remember her. "She wrote in the Writer's Room. I saw her sometimes, we said hello. When I saw that sign I thought about how easily it could have been the other way around, that she could have lived and I could have died and she would have come in and looked at a sign that said how sad everyone was about Lucy Grealy committing suicide. And Ann, I felt so unbelievably lucky to be alive. I walked outside and the world was just incredibly beautiful to me. I cried I was so happy. I really do want to be alive."

*Death destroys a man but the Idea of Death can save him*, she added on the bottom of a letter. *I just read this & I liked it.*

AROUND THIS TIME things in my life were taking an unexpected turn. My novel, *Bel Canto*, which had chugged along with moderate sales during its year in hardback, had suddenly become a best seller in paperback. It won a prize in the States and then in England. My fourth book made me an overnight success. Over the past few years I had seen many of my friends come to glory. Elizabeth had been nominated for a National Book Award and then won a prize from the Academy of Arts and Letters. My friend Manette had a book that was chosen for Oprah Winfrey's book club. Adrian's book that was ten years in the making was published to the biggest avalanche of acclaim I had ever seen and had a front-page review in the *New York Times*. And Lucy, Lucy had led the way for all of us. Now it seemed it was me.

Lucy was happy for me. She worked at being happy for me. "It's not that I'm not jealous," she said, "but my pride in you is much bigger than my jealousy. Anyway, I called this one. I told you this was your best book."

I saw Lucy that spring when I was giving a reading in New York. She was supposed to come with Karl and me to the Museum of Natural History to see the butterfly exhibit that day but she decided at the last minute that it was too impossible to come uptown and she would meet us for dinner. She still had a large band of swelling on her neck and she was wearing a turtleneck sweater. She always wore turtlenecks after surgeries and though I bought them for her all the time, I rarely got the right one. There was a very specific way they had to sit on her neck to be both comfortable and effective for their purpose. "What do you think of my face?" she said.

We were in Balthazar, near her old apartment in SoHo, which kindly paints everyone in a warm orange glow, but even in flattering light Lucy's face seemed frozen somehow, as if she were wearing a clay mask. Or maybe it was only that I wasn't used to it yet. It was such a different face from the one I'd seen the last time. It seemed so immobile. "I think you look good," I said.

"Fuck good!" she said. "I didn't go through all of this so that I could look good. I want to look great."

"You look great," I said.

"It doesn't count now."

"Please," I said, "forgive me. You look great."

The next night we all went together to an awards ceremony. I was a finalist for a literary prize and Lucy met us at the hotel. Karl took me aside and told me he thought she was drunk or high, but that couldn't be possible since she had told me she was completely clean. A lot of people were there that night who wanted my attention for one reason or another, but whenever anyone came up to try and speak to me, Lucy would step between us and pull down my head so that she could tap her forehead against mine.

"You're such a rock star."

"Hardly."

"Do you love me?" she asked.

"I do love you."

She put her arms around my neck and hung there. "You're going to win," she said. "You're the best." If I turned my eyes away from her, she would put her hands on my head and tilt it towards her again. "Didn't I tell you this was a great book?"

I lost the prize and my publisher and agent took us out to dinner in a gesture of good sportsmanship. There were seven of us at the table and Lucy sat beside me. Whenever someone said anything to me, she would start to whisper in my ear.

"Bastards," she said. "You should have won. You were robbed." She ordered another Cosmopolitan.

"It's okay," I said.

She pressed her head against my shoulder and looked up at me. "Do you love me?" She threw one leg over mine and in doing so managed to swallow up all the air in the restaurant. She kept it up all through dinner, through dessert, through the walk down the street to find her a cab. Karl gave her twenty dollars for her fare, kissed her good night, and sent her home.

A week later she pulled her car into a parking lot in Pittsfield, Massachusetts, on her way home from Bennington in the middle of the night, cut herself with razor blades, drank, took a handful of pills, and passed out. A policeman found her and took her to the local hospital, where she spent the night. Her voice was stripped from vomiting in the car but we talked for an hour, and the next day we talked for an hour again. She told me in a whisper that she was sorry, that she loved me, that she didn't mean to hurt me, that she could not stand to live in this present state of loneliness anymore. She said everything I knew, and then I told her everything she knew, that I loved her and would do anything I could for her and that if she would just come to Nashville, just for a while, and live in her room, I could at least help her until she was on her feet. I knew that nothing either one of us said could change anything but I was just so grateful to hear her voice, talking.

"I keep thinking that if I keep doing this someone is going to see how much pain I'm in and they're going to help me," she whispered.

"I can help you," I said. "Let me."

"I don't know how," she said sadly.

When Bennington fired her a month later for missing so many classes, she was a little nervous but mostly thrilled. She said she was relieved to have the pressure taken off, and now that she didn't have to do all that driving, everything would be easier. "This is going to make all the difference. I already feel a hundred times better." But her book contract, the subject of so many discussions and extensions, had finally been canceled in December. I wasn't sure how much there was left to give up.

                                *    *    *

I MET HER A WEEK later at the Park Avenue Café for dinner. I wanted
to take her someplace nice, but when she looked around she said the
restaurant was full of tourists.

"How can you tell?"

"Just look at them," she said. "Look at what they're eating." She
ordered a glass of wine and I asked her not to, not that a glass of wine
made one bit of difference in the world, I just didn't want to watch her
drink it.

Lucy told me to lighten up. She was in a good mood that night. She
was loving without being clinging, she was talkative. She said that
being fired was just what she had needed. It opened up so much for her.
Now she would be able to go back to work on her book and maybe she
wouldn't even try to get Doubleday to pick up the contract again.
Maybe she would sell it for more money someplace else. It might not
even be a novel. She might really write the book about her friends. She
was also about to be evicted from her beloved apartment, which was a
sublet, but maybe she'd find something even better. "I don't have to
worry about it all right now."

"What about the drugs?"

She rolled her eyes, not because I was asking, but as a way of saying
those pesky drugs were still in the picture. "I'm working on it."

My hands were sweating. Sitting there over a pricey piece of half-
eaten fish, I felt as if I had suddenly turned a corner. "Lucy," I said.

"Yes, pet?"

"You know I've seen you through a lot of things. I've always stuck
by you." I was shaking. I surprised myself by shaking. "But I can't
stand this. I can barely explain it to you, but I feel a revulsion for what
you're doing. All these years I've watched these things hurt you, things

you had no control over, and now to have to watch you hurt yourself, it's too much for me."

She tilted her head and gave me the warmest, loveliest smile. "I'm sorry," she said.

I put my hands flat on the table and stared at the heavy silverware touching my thumbs. I kept my eyes down when I should have looked at her. "I'll leave you over this," I said. "I mean it. Someday soon I'll come to the end of my rope and I won't be able to help you anymore."

"I know," she said, and she leaned across the table and kissed me. "I love you for saying this. It means the world to me."

I looked at her, blinking. I wasn't expecting this. I thought she would at least tell me I was wrong about everything.

"Sophie pretty much said the same thing, and Joy. It makes me love all of you so much."

I wondered how Sophie and Joy had felt, if their hands had shaken, too. Lucie B-B was different. She didn't approve of Lucy's behavior, but she offered her a friendship that was completely free of judgment. There was no part of Lucy she turned away from. Her love was based on unwavering acceptance.

Lucy tapped her finger on the back of my hand. "Just don't leave me yet," she said. "Give me a little more time to try."

I loved her insanely at that moment. There was something about her composure, her little request, that completely broke my heart. I knew I could never draw a line I would not be willing to erase later on. "Of course I won't leave you yet," I said.

I saw her again a few days later at Café des Artistes. Karl had invited some of my friends for drinks before I went to give a talk at Lincoln Center with Renée Fleming. But Lucy was strung out again, scattered and demanding. She hadn't eaten all day and she wanted a milkshake. She was irritated that the restaurant was too fancy to come up with a milkshake, so Artie and Adrian left the party and took her to a diner down the street to settle her down. It was impossible for me to tell when she was high and when she was coming off being high and when she was just in a foul temper.

*Bel Canto* was keeping me out of the house and on the road. It seemed like every third week I was in New York. Sometimes Lucy was awful and sometimes she was good. When I saw her at the end of May, she said she thought she was coming out of her depression. She told me she had been clean for twenty-eight days. She was talking again about going to medical school. Lucy had been premed in college and whenever writing seemed impossible she toyed around with the idea of going back to the love of her childhood. She wanted to be like William Carlos Williams, a writing doctor. Normally the whole thing was a lark, something you say when work was going badly, but this time she was much more serious. She didn't want to teach anymore. She didn't want to have to make a living at writing, she wanted to keep it as an art. The discipline of school would be good for her, and she would get to meet a whole new group of people.

"Young people," I said. "Very young people."

"They have students my age."

She had met with the people in the intensive premed programs at Hunter and Columbia and they were encouraging. The woman at Columbia had read Lucy's book and was anxious to help her.

"What about the money?" I said.

"It's $20,000. I could write a few articles to pay for the classes."

"But what about the money for medical school?" After all, she was still being hunted down for both her graduate and undergraduate loans in addition to back taxes. I didn't think the government would come through for her this time.

Lucy waved me off. "That's the least of my problems. If I find a way to do this and I get in then I'll just get somebody else to pay for it."

I was wondering if she meant me. Do they let suicidal heroin addicts into medical school, I wanted to ask her, but I kept my mouth shut.

When Lucy finally lost her apartment in the National Arts Club, she was thrown off track again. Without the Bennington job, all she could afford was a place she found in Brooklyn and even though it was close to Joy's, she considered her move to the boroughs as an exile to Siberia. Her sister Sarah and Sarah's husband Bob had been working hard to unsnarl the financial knot that Lucy lived in, and had cosigned their names to her lease, as Lucy's credit history was like a cautionary tale of how everything can go wrong. Lucy hated the place. She complained about all the walking she had to do and her leg was giving her no end of pain, for which she had no end of narcotics. She blamed herself for her leg, thinking that she had embarked on surgical folly and had wound up worse off than before. She was completely, wretchedly miserable, but then told me after the fact it was because she had been on a huge heroin bender before she moved and decided that she would quit cold turkey when she got to Brooklyn. But I didn't know that at the time. I pictured her world as she described it to me: a mile from the subway, no grocery store, no hardware store, nothing but endless buildings that all looked exactly the same.

The apartment she left in the city had a furnished kitchen and out in Brooklyn she had neither spoon nor coffee cup to her name. The move and the drugs had used up her money and energy and she sat on the floor, surrounded by boxes, and cried.

"I can set up your kitchen," I said. "At least I can do that. I'll order it. I'll have it shipped. You don't even have to go outside." I wouldn't

give Lucy money anymore, but I'd buy her things or send an emergency
rent check directly to her landlord. After we talked for an hour, I went
online and bought her everything I could think of: pot holders and veg-
etable peelers and plates and pans. The order came in six different ship-
ments. I bought her Tupperware. It was my own special brand of
insanity that made me think the trials of Lucy's life could somehow be
eased by the order of Tupperware.

One day in the middle of the summer, Lucy's doctor, Stuart, called
me. As soon as I heard his voice, my heart froze in my chest. I leaned
my head back against the wall where I stood and closed my eyes.
"Lucy's dead," I said.

"What!" Stuart said.

"There's only one reason you'd call me."

It turned out there were two reasons: Stuart and his girlfriend were
coming to Tennessee on vacation and he wanted some advice about
places to see. We laughed about it because everything was fine, but for
the rest of the day I felt cold.

I started hearing from Lucy less and less again. She wouldn't return
my calls. The worse things got, the more she avoided me: I was too
judgmental; she hated to disappoint me; both things were true. When
she finally surfaced again at the end of the summer, she had been using
for two months solid and was just coming out of it. The difference was,
this time she knew for sure: it was over. You couldn't pay her to use
heroin again. Before she had never been absolutely positive, but this
was something else entirely.

SHE LEFT BROOKLYN. She had been fired from her job in the low-
residency graduate program and was out of money and anyway, she
hated Brooklyn. She said she had gotten the dates of the premed

program wrong and so she'd already missed the first two classes. She thought it was better to wait and start in the winter term. She moved out to a farm in Connecticut to live with her childhood friend, Stephen. He also kept a tiny rent-controlled apartment on the Upper East Side and it gave Lucy a place to go when she wanted to spend the night in the city. In the autumn she went there and left a message on Lucie B-B's answering machine. She was going to kill herself by taking an overdose of heroin. Lucie was in Cambridge when she picked up the message from New York, but she called Sophie, who remembered the phone number at Stephen's apartment and so with a little bit of fast Internet work was able to figure out the address. Since neither of them was in the city, they called Lucy's friend Ben in the middle of the night, who rushed over to find Lucy sick and high and wide awake, the door unlocked, shooting heroin.

Joy was the one who called me. Joy always got stuck with the psych ward duty. She had lost a sister when she was five, two of her best friends had died in accidents, and her father had died the year before. She sat in Lucy's room at the hospital and told her that she just wasn't up to having to sort through another dead friend's things.

"I kept telling her, I can't believe I'm sitting here, having this conversation with you and you're going to be dead," Joy said to me over the phone.

"Lucy's not going to die," I said. Suddenly I was angry. "These are candy-ass suicide attempts. She may wind up homeless. She may alienate everyone she knows, but she isn't going to die. Lucy will be the last one of us left standing." Life had been conspiring to kill Lucy since she was ten years old and life had failed. At every turn she wrestled with death. She always won.

"She looked me right in the face," Joy said. "She told me she wished she'd succeeded."

The next night I talked to Lucy from the pay phone for a long time. It was cold and bright in Nashville and I stood outside in my backyard and looked up at the stars. Lucy told me she was going into rehab in Connecticut. In the middle of all the talk about fresh starts and new jobs, we started talking about Nabokov, and then we were talking about the night sky, the different sides we saw from New York and Tennessee, and then about the metaphysical process of sight. She told me she had just found out that stevensite was actually named for a man named Stevens, who had discovered it.

"I don't even know what stevensite is."

"It's a mineral," she told me.

"Who will I talk to if you keep going like this?" I wanted to know. "Who will there be for me to talk to?"

"I'll get over this," she said. "We'll look back and call these the heroin years. We'll say, 'Do you remember when Lucy was a heroin addict?'"

"We thought it was very serious," I said.

"We thought she was gone for good," Lucy said, "but then something happened, no one ever knew what it was, but one day she straightened back up. When you look at how wonderful her life is now, you can hardly even believe it was really her."

## Chapter Eighteen

LUCY STAYED IN REHAB OUT IN CONNECTICUT FOR A
while and then went back to Stephen's to do the rest of the program as an outpatient. She was as sullen as a ninth-grader sent to summer school to repeat algebra.

"I'm not like those people," she told me. "I'm not an addict."

"For God's sake, if you won't even admit that you're an addict,
then why are you doing this?"

"For my friends," she said. "So my friends will trust me again and
get off my back."

"You don't do rehab for your friends."

"Well, I guess it's possible since that's what I'm doing. It's complete
bullshit, even the whole twelve-step thing, 'We believe in a higher
power.' I just said to them, 'You can't expect me to believe there's a
God just because you tell me there's a God.' I'm supposed to put aside
a thousand years of philosophy just because some social worker tells
me that there's a God?"

"So now you're the smartest person in rehab."

"I'll quit using drugs because I want to quit."

"Have you quit?"

"Of course I have," she said. She was furious. We were both furious. She got pneumonia again and wound up in the hospital but checked herself out a day later against doctor's orders. They were Connecticut doctors. They had no idea what in the hell they were talking about.

"I have to move back into the city," she said. "I need to be back with my friends."

"You can't move back. You don't have any money. You're in terrible health. You've got to just lie low for a while, take care of yourself." I thought of Andy, who was desperately trying to keep Lucy out of the city, away from her dealer. He thought there had to be a place in the world where she wouldn't be able to get her hands on drugs.

"I can live in Stephen's apartment. It's less expensive to live in the city if you know what you're doing."

I was always telling her no. No and wait and stay where you are. No had become my habit with Lucy and it seemed like especially good advice now that every step forward looked like it was straight off a cliff.


I WAS COMING to the city in December to go to a movie premier and the Christmas party at the *New York Times*. I didn't tell Lucy because she would have wanted to come and if she had come, she would have ruined it for me. Karl and I were only going to be there two nights, and I wanted to have some fun. It would be the first time I had ever gone to the city and not told Lucy I was there. A few hours before I left, she called me.

"I got you!" she said.

"Have you been trying to get me? I've left you a dozen messages and you never call me back."

"I don't like your answering machine," Lucy said. "I won't talk to it." I had just gotten a new machine with a standard electronic voice instead of my voice so that the crazy strangers who had started calling me would be unsure as to whether or not they had the right number. I explained this to her but she didn't care. "I'm only going to talk to you in person until you change your message."

I almost told her, I'm coming to New York today and we can meet for dinner tonight, but I didn't say anything.

"I was thinking of coming to Nashville for Christmas," she said.

"I'll be in Atlanta."

"Then maybe I'll come and spend Christmas with your mother. I'd like to hang out with your mother."

"You can call her," I said, "but Christmas is two weeks away."

"It would probably be hard to get a ticket," she said sadly. "But I miss you so much."

"The important thing is you're getting better." It was a mean thing to say. I didn't miss her. And I needed to pack.

"Are you saying you don't miss me?"

"Of course I miss you."

"I love you," she said wistfully, sweetly.

"I love you, too," I said. I did, though at the moment it was a rushed sort of love.

There was a pause on the line and then Lucy sighed. "Okay, then. I guess I should go. We should talk more often. We should start talking every day again."

"We should," I said. "We're better when we talk every day."

After I hung up the phone, it rang a minute later.

"You think I'm talented, don't you?" Lucy said.

"Of course I think you're talented."

"Okay. I was just checking. Good-bye again."

And then she was gone.

*For some strange reason birds keep crashing into my window* [she had written to me from Aberdeen in 1990]. *The second one just bonked into it while I was sitting here, and two did yesterday also. Maybe it's an omen (didn't I write a poem with birds crashing into windows once?) I remember it now: it was a bad omen in the poem. Do you ever have premonitions? I have black empty ones all the time, not of a bad future, but of no future. It scares me a great deal, I can't describe it, but it feels so certain. I like to think it is only my imagination, a result of my depression.*

We came back from New York on December 18, 2002, a Wednesday afternoon. When Stuart called me at ten-thirty that night, I was already asleep. This time he was calling to say that Lucy was dead. His voice was surprised and afraid. He wasn't sure of the sentence himself. "Ann," he said. "Lucy's dead." When I hung up the phone I gave myself a few minutes in the dark to lie in bed and pretend I had been dreaming. He still had my number programmed into his cellphone from his trip to Tennessee, so when he heard from the medical examiner, I was the first person he called. I called Joy, who called Sophie, who called Lucie, and from there the phone calls made their rounds. When the phone call reached Stephen to tell him Lucy was dead, he said he knew because he was sitting on the bed with her body and the police were there. It was Stephen who had gone looking for her when she didn't return his calls and it was Stephen who had found her in his little apartment in the city.

At three o'clock in the morning, I drove to Karl's house and when I woke him up and told him what I knew I started to cry, because I had just begun the second half of my life, the half that would be lived without Lucy.

\*　　\*　　\*

WHEN THE CORONER'S REPORT came back weeks later we were told that while she had heroin in her system, it was not a lethal dosage. There was food on the table, and she was in bed. She had not asphyxiated, as everyone had thought at first. All I knew for sure was that she was dead. What combination of things brought that about would be impossible to say. Still, I took a little comfort thinking maybe she was not so terribly unhappy in that moment. Maybe she was sleepy and full and pleasantly high and had just crawled beneath her blanket to sleep. Her death was ruled an accidental overdose.

I can manage to conjure up all sorts of alternate scenarios, my favorite being the one in which I take her with me to the parties in New York. She wears the silvery silk cocktail dress with the full skirt and everyone is so glad to see her and she has a wonderful time, so she thinks she'll put the heroin off for a little while because, after all, I'm around, and so she lives for another week, and because she is feeling stronger, she lives for the week after that as well. She goes on for a month, and then a year. I try not to be greedy. I try to tell myself not to ask for more than a year, and then I wonder who it is I'm asking. She is dead, and I have nothing to ask for at all. The truth is I would have settled for a week. In that time I would have found my patience again. It had come back to me a hundred times before. That was part of Lucy's genius in having so many friends. We all lost our patience with her, but never at the same time. If one of us was tired, there was always someone else to pick up the lamp and lead her home. It would have been me again, I know that. There was a time, just a moment that night in the Park Avenue Café, I had thought I could let her go. But now I know I was simply not cut out for life without her. I am living that life now and would not choose it. If Lucy couldn't give up the heroin, I could not give up Lucy.

Most nights I dream of her. I am in a strange city and I see her sitting in a café, drinking coffee and writing in a notebook. She is frail beyond anything I could have imagined, barely able to pick up her cup with two hands, but she's happy to see me. I run to her, kiss her, and she pulls herself up in my arms to sit in my lap and curl against me like a little bird.

"I thought you were dead," I say, joyful because there she is, still alive, still mine. I wrap my arms around her, her forehead pressing into the curve of my neck. "Everyone thinks that you're dead."

"I had to try to get better one more time," she says, her voice tired. "I just didn't want to put everyone through it again, me trying to pull myself together, me failing." She tells me she is in a very secret rehab. It is only for people who everyone thinks are already dead. There is only a fifty-fifty chance of her making it, but if she got through the program she would be clean and well forever. "I figure this way if I die no one will know it, no one will have to go through all that sadness again, and if I live I'll be absolutely better and then everyone will be so happy to see me."

"We'd be happy to see you no matter how you are."

"Trust me," she says, touching my wrist.

In the dark bar, which might have been Café Drummond in Aberdeen, she is on my lap and I am tearing up tiny bites of croissants filled with almond paste and feeding them to her, when I suddenly remember something. "Oh my God, Lucy, I'm writing a book about you being dead." I feel embarrassed somehow, as if this proves I had lost faith in her ability to still be alive. "I'm so sorry. I'll throw it away."

Lucy shakes her head. I could feel her in my arms, just the weight of her bones, the brush of her head against my cheek. "Go ahead and write it," she says. "I'll probably die. Even if I don't die now, I'll die sooner or later, right?"

Night after night after night I find her, always in a public place, a museum, a restaurant, on a train. Every night she's glad to see me and she folds into my arms. But each time there is less of her to hold on to. I could see her kindness in letting people think she's dead. It was going to be horrible to lose her again. As time passes I see her less often in my dreams, though she would still call me from the secret rehab. They weren't letting her out anymore, she tells me, but she's allowed to call me since I already know the truth. In this little way I am allowed to visit my dead.

ONE NIGHT, when we were in our early twenties and still living in Iowa, we went to the campus theater to see a showing of Cocteau's *Orpheus*. We sat with a group of poets, friends of Lucy's, and together we cheered the scenes in the Poet's Café where fistfights broke out over the scribbled drafts of a few new poems. I remember it as being a wonderful night. The movie thrilled us, and we walked home in the bitter cold talking about how brilliant Cocteau had been to make a movie in which the poets were the most important and revered people in society. Lucy said she was in love with Heurtebise, who played the part of Death's driver. She thought it showed a great sensibility on her part to fall for the sidekick, the number-two man, instead of wanting Orpheus for herself, who, with his enormous beauty would have been perhaps too ambitious a choice. I agreed with her completely about the appeal of Heurtebise, although the sight of Orpheus asleep in the sand, his cheek pressed against a mirror, was one that would stay with me for years.

"You should take Orpheus, then," she said.

"But I loved Heurtebise, too," I said, and it was true. I did. And I also didn't want Lucy to feel like she was settling. "He had a greater soul than Orpheus."

She shook her head. "It just seemed that way because he was already dead. Really, take Orpheus."

We were two young women talking about which of the dead French movie stars we would have rather gone on a date with. In short, we were very much alive.

After Lucy died, all I could think of was seeing that movie again. It had stuck in my head as the only source of available comfort. After all, who had any leverage with Death except Orpheus? Who had ever been beautiful enough and clever enough to cut a deal? I was remembering the myth, that Orpheus's love for Eurydice was so great that he went down to the underworld to lead her out, only to lose her again when he broke the one rule: Don't look back.

But once I saw the film I remembered that that wasn't Cocteau's story at all. In his version, Orpheus wasn't really so interested in Eurydice, who was beautiful and fair and pregnant, the very light of life itself. Orpheus was in love with Death, who was angular and dark, with a waist small enough to be encircled by two human hands. It was Death he was hoping to see when he went back for his wife; it was Death he kissed and made promises to. I had to wonder if that was the part of the story that Lucy remembered. She had a nearly romantic relationship with Death. She had beaten it out so many times that she was convinced she could go and kiss all she wanted and still come out on the other side. Even when she wanted to die she couldn't seem to pull it off. Lucy, weighing about a hundred pounds, having survived thirty-eight operations, had become officially invincible. She believed that the most basic rules of life did not apply to her, and over the course of our friendship, without me knowing when it had happened, I had come to believe it myself. The sheer force of Lucy's life convinced me that she would live no matter what.

That was my mistake.